The HOME BUTCHER

The *HOME* BUTCHER

Simple, Modern Techniques for Processing Beef, Lamb, Sheep & Goat, Pork, Poultry & Fowl, Rabbit, Venison & Other Game

James O. Fraioli

Skyhorse Publishing

Visit our website at www.skyhorsepublishing.com.

10 9 8 7 6 5 4 3 2

Library of Congress Cataloging-in-Publication Data is available on file.

Cover design by Laura Klynstra
Cover illustrations: iStock.

Print ISBN: 978-1-5107-4579-7
Ebook ISBN: 978-1-5107-4580-3

Printed in China

Contents

Introduction

Almost every time we sit at a dinner table, a protein is the center of attention. Whether that is a roasted leg of lamb, a lovely beef Wellington, or a simple roasted chicken, these meats catch our eye, our senses, and our culinary palate. They feed us, nourish our families, and sustain us. Often the dinner conversation will wander to "Where did you find this chicken breast? It's so tender and juicy!" or "How did you cook these lamb shanks? They're delicious!" This incredible satisfaction, along with the connection to the particular cut of meat, is where the story of home butchering begins.

History

The art of butchery began a very long time ago, evidenced by the simple forms of butchery in prehistoric times. It is thought that the practice of hunting and breaking down animals was a large leap in the evolution of humankind. Later,

THE SHOP OF CASTRO THE BUTCHER AT WAGGA WAGGA

the Roman era advanced the process when the chopping block and cleaver were first created, making the dressing of meats and sharing the bounty at large banquets popular. It didn't take long until butchery was at the forefront and butchers were highly praised, becoming pillars of their communities.

However, the profession truly began to take shape when livestock became domesticated and the urban migration began, creating the demand for meat as towns and cities quickly grew. Butchery continued to be one of the most reputable professions, and the butcher continued to garner respect. AD 975 is the date of one of the earliest references to butchers as we know them today, and during the fourteenth century, the Worshipful Company of Butchers Guild was formed. The company remains one of the oldest guilds in the United Kingdom, one in which discussions surrounding techniques for creating primal cuts from a carcass began. In many ways, it was during this time the butchering industry became standardized and even more specialized, in hopes of creating the best and most complete use of the animal. The butchers' focus was a high level of care and cleanliness with the animals as well as ensuring the best flavor and proper cuts to meet customer satisfaction.

Today, the art of butchering has changed little, even though heading to the local butcher to purchase your Sunday roast and daily staples has, in many ways, turned into a supermarket run with little interaction with the butchers themselves. The desire for traceability, knowing our food and where it comes from, as well as a continued respect for the animals that sustain us, has renewed a desire to bring this ancient practice back into the home.

Revival of Home Butchering Today

Bringing the art of butchering back into the home is multifaceted and to be celebrated. There is nothing better than appreciating the beautiful animal that was successfully raised or hunted by hosting a large gathering for family and friends, just as the Romans did. Together, we butcher the deer, store it away for the winter, knowing that we all have plenty to eat for the months to come. Along with the gathering of friends and family, purchasing a whole animal and butchering at home while sharing the cost makes the entire process much more economical. It demonstrates the desire to not waste anything—and nose-to-tail eating means bones for broth, and quality organ meat too. Often, supermarkets won't take the time to get the more difficult cuts of meat, even if they are some of the most tender and flavorful. The lack of transparency with supermarket meat is yet another impetus to bring the practice again into the home.

Delicious meals come from the best ingredients, and sourcing quality meat is the most important component of home butchering. Finding trusted local farmers and learning about their animals, farm, and feed practices are foundational for home butchery. Having the opportunity to visit the farm and talk to the farmer will allow you to further understand how the animals are being treated, what they are being fed, and the entire growing process.

An important distinction to note is that between grass fed and grass finished, especially for beef and lamb. With grass fed, the animal has a primary diet of grass as they spend their days in pasture, although the final thirty days before slaughter the animal could be "finished" with grain. A grass-finished animal could consume grain or a combination of grass and grain for most of its life and only be fed grass in its final thirty days before slaughter. Asking the farmer about diet is important, as this will reflect highly in the flavor of the animal. Pasture-raised animals are known to contain less fat and have more complex flavor as they live most of their lives in a natural habitat.

A similar situation for pork is also of note. An important designation is outdoor bred compared to outdoor reared. Outdoor bred pigs are born outdoors and allowed to be with the herd when they are young. As soon as they are weaned, they are brought indoors for fattening. Outdoor-reared pigs, meanwhile, spend more than half their life outdoors. Asking about diet is important, as pigs are often fed scraps of all kinds, and their feed will change the meat tremendously. Will the pigs be eating leftover apples from a cider mill or commercial feed? The more detail you can glean from a farmer the more you will learn to aid your home butchering experience while truly understanding the

animals that you're bringing into your home to sustain you for months.

Poultry is yet another learning experience. If wanting to raise a backyard flock, there are many resources available to help ensure your feed and diet formulation are keeping your flock growing and healthy. When talking to a farmer about their flock, with the intention to purchase a bird to butcher at home, asking questions about the feed is important. Feed contains many different grains and proteins as well as vitamins and nutrients. If a chicken is organically grown, the feed ingredients should not be genetically modified and should not contain animal products, such as bone meal or fish meal, as a source of nutrients.

When looking for meat at butcher shops, finding US Department of Agriculture–certified cuts is often important when quality is the intention. Organic and other related programs offered by the USDA are carcass certifications, not animal, so asking the farmer if they are involved in any auditing or verification program is the best first step to understanding if the animal would be considered certified after slaughter. The programs offered are vast and varied, especially in terms of final meat quality, so having further conversations with the farmer is best before deciding on which animal to butcher.

Researching the best areas for hunting, the wilderness landscape, and learning from experienced hunters is also foundational for sourcing game. Contacting state wildlife agencies is a great way to understand where to find the game you're looking for, the best time in a season to hunt, as well as where the best public lands are found to pursue the game. From understanding how controlled hunts and limited draws happen, as well as the use of preference points, the hunting of game can be just as challenging as finding a quality farmer to raise animals naturally.

Understanding the traceability of the animals and ultimately the meat and story of the people who raised them brings the process full circle, creating space at the table to share the story of what you are truly enjoying.

Optimal Workspace

Creating a perfect workspace when butchering at home is important for each aspect of the butchering process. Ensuring the counters and work surfaces are clean and organized helps keeps the process running smoothly and efficiently while also ensuring the meat is preserved to the best of your ability. The best cleaning products, from salt and lemon or vinegar and water, to more chemical-based cleaners and bleach, all have their part in keeping your surfaces sanitized. Using natural cleaners on wood is best as it is porous; soaking a cutting board in lemon juice and salting it overnight will prevent bacteria from growing as quickly when using a board over the course of a day. Washing knives and tools when switching between cuts, and keeping surfaces wiped clean as you work, will also keep your surface as clean as possible.

Sharpening knives and tools the day before you plan to butcher is a good practice, as is keeping essential tools close at hand. Arranging your knives and tools in order of use, and from the most used to least used, is also important when butchering so nothing is not far from reach. Wearing a designated apron or work coat also helps keep the area clean and prevents the transfer of bacteria to other areas of your kitchen or

home. Washing your apron in hot water when changing types of meat as well as when you're finished for the day will also keep bacteria from wandering and causing cross contamination.

After all your meat is wrapped and stored, disinfect all your cutting boards, counters, and surfaces as if you're just beginning. Splatters can reach farther than expected, and keeping a kitchen clean is the foundation of ensuring that every meal is prepared to food-safe best practices.

Before butchering, dry or wet aging your meat is a best practice to ensure that the connective tissue has a chance to break down and the muscle fibers have time to denature. It's also important to ensure that the meat stays a consistent 34 to 37°F for the days or weeks that the meat ages. Wet aging is usually easiest for the home butcher as the wet aging process happens after the meat has been butchered and allowed to thaw. Keep the meat in its vacuum sealed bag for up to two weeks after it's removed from the freezer. Dry aging requires larger hanging spaces as the meat needs to be hung in large pieces before the butchering and preserving process is finished. This is easy for a commercial butchery with a walk-in fridge, although most home butchers don't have that luxury.

Refrigerator and Freezer Space

Labeling and creating your own best-practice system for storage in the refrigerator and

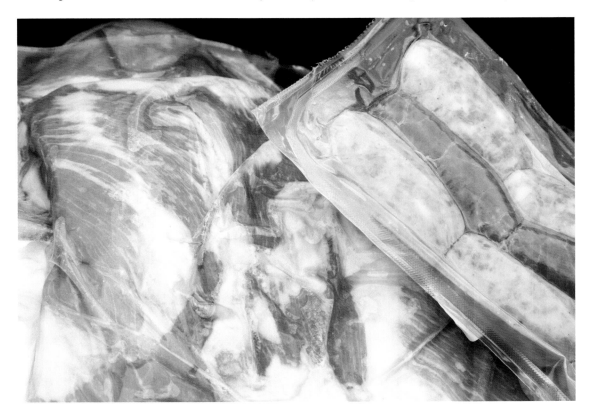

freezer is important to ensure that nothing goes to waste. Place cuts of meat that need to be used first on the top right of the freezer and larger cuts in the bottom left. Rotating through your meat helps prevent freezer burn and the inevitable reality of cuts being lost in the bottom of the freezer. Packaging by portion size, based on your family's typical eating habits, ensures that what is hawed will be consumed. Erring on the side of smaller package portions—for example, two steaks are better than six—is best practice so you don't thaw more than you need that day.

Proper Packaging and Storage

Vacuum-sealing meat, especially poultry, rabbit, and smaller game, is preferable as it prevents meat from being exposed to the air for long periods of time. Freezer-burned flesh doesn't cook well and has an unsatisfactory taste, and all the natural moisture from the meat has evaporated. Vacuum-sealing is also preferable for larger cuts of game if wet aging is desired, although this method can be challenging as excess liquid in the vacuum bag can ruin the seal. Otherwise, for large cuts of meat, butcher paper works perfectly well. Wrapping

the meat twice prevents freezer burn and is also much more economical when working with larger animals.

Using a Sharpie-style marker will ensure that dates don't freeze off and won't bleed through to the meat. Write on the paper or bag before the meat is added as temperature changes can cause the marker to smudge before the ink is set. Always use freezer tape or string to close the packages; masking tape or duct tape will come loose in the cold freezer. On each package, write the cut of meat, date and use-by date, as well as any additional storage information or what you'd like to use the meat for ("beef strips for stir-fry"). This will help prevent mystery meat from appearing a year later, and cuts not being used at their optimal time.

When storing meat in the refrigerator, place in a bottom drawer. This keeps other fresh ingredients in your refrigerator safe and clean from any bleeding or dripping and ensures a more consistent and cooler temperature. Keeping the same labeling system and rotation in both the refrigerator and the freezer is also a best practice.

For a complete list of tools and equipment needed for butchering, please refer to the individual chapters, which outline the knives and tools needed for each animal.

Meat and Wine Pairings

After the butchering process is complete and all your hard work is tucked in the freezer, the second part of the story begins. Preparing and enjoying all the delicious cuts of meat, from brining and marinating to quick searing and roasting—the possibilities are virtually endless. This book is filled with recipes, ideas, and suggestions. Each dish is also paired with wine, a process that is an art unto itself.

A traditional rule of thumb: the color of meat should be paired with the like color of wine. This rule is a basic premise, although it doesn't always hold true. A rich delicious beef tenderloin needs a wine to stand up to it, not something that will hide or disappear behind the flavor of the meat. Therefore, a Chardonnay or Riesling probably won't be the best to pair, while a Cabernet Sauvignon, Bordeaux blend, or Zinfandel would bring out the brightness and richness of the meat and complement it perfectly. On the flip side, a tender rabbit loin would be overpowered by a rich bold red wine, so a buttery Chardonnay would be delightful.

Always consider the sauces and sides that you're serving with the meal as well, as this can also influence the perfect pairing. Chicken in a richly spiced tomato sauce would pair exceptionally well with a Pinot Noir or Beaujolais nouveau, while a pork tenderloin seared and served with an apple or fruit sauce would be better served by a sauvignon blanc or Gewürztraminer. Tasting the wine before serving and tasting the similar qualities between the dishes and the meat is the best way to ensure the pairing is ideal. Finding familiar grape varietals also helps ensure that your wine won't overpower the food, and vice versa. The reality is, perfect pairings do enhance a dish, although the best wine is the one you like the most.

From sourcing your animal and butchering at home, to enjoying a delicious meal around the table, this book is a comprehensive guide to home butchering, cooking the cuts you've stored, and sharing the experience among friends and family, over—what else of course, but a wonderful glass of wine.

Salut!

Butchering
Chicken & Other Birds

In this chapter, we will delve into the process of dispatching and butchering a chicken using an easy-to-follow, step-by-step bullet-point breakdown, which you can adjust and apply to other culinary birds, such as turkey, duck, pheasant, and goose. As you will soon discover, the slaughtering and butchering of birds is far less complex than the larger animals we will explore in the chapters ahead—animals that take a much more substantial amount of time and preparation to go from carcass to finished cuts, but the results will be the same as those larger animals.

Butchering tools and equipment:

- Sharp kitchen or butcher's knife.
- Sharp kitchen knife with slim point or deboning knife.
- Sharp ax or hatchet.
- Large pot and heat source to heat water.
- Bucket to remove guts.
- Water source. Ideally a hose but also a bucket of water.
- A vinegar solution spray of 2.5 percent vinegar to water (optional) for cleaning purposes.
- Clean bucket for the meat.
- Table surface or cutting board.
- Moist towel.
- Sharp kitchen shears (for butchering quail).
- Organic acid rinse, optional (for butchering quail).
- Ziplock bags (for butchering quail).

Words of Caution:

It's critical that you take knife safety seriously when processing chicken and other small birds.

You have probably heard people say never cut toward yourself. True, but because chicken and many game birds are small, you tend to be working with your hands very close to each other. Therefore, it's critical that you are aware of your knife at all times. There are two general practices to instill into your butchering practice. The first is holding the knife the entire time you're processing. The second is having a table close to you so that when you're not processing, you can set the knife in a safe secure place where you won't accidentally cut yourself.

Slaughter techniques:

- To begin, simply grasp the chicken by its feet and legs and invert the chicken upside down so the head and neck are toward the ground. Having someone assist by holding the chicken for you, including pinning back the wings, will make the slaughtering process easier.
- Slice the knife across the throat under the chin on either side of the larynx. Make one parallel cut on each side of the neck. This will sever the arteries and not the trachea. As the chicken quickly bleeds out, there will be involuntary twitching or thrashing about, for around one minute. This is normal during the slaughtering process, but rest assured the animal is being killed humanely.
- Another slaughter method is incorporating the use of a sharp ax or hatchet. This is a much easier slaughter method, but not always the cleanest and visually pleasing.
- Have someone hold the chicken down on a chopping block and keep holding the animal until it is calm.

- With a sharp hatchet, and being extremely careful of the assistant's hands and arms, perform a strong swing and sever the chicken's head completely from its body. Again, there will be involuntary twitching and thrashing about, for around one minute. This is normal during the slaughtering process.
- An additional slaughtering method, one that does not involve any tools or bloodshed, is using your hands to break the chicken's neck. Breaking the neck must be carried out with force and without hesitation. This method is not recommended for amateur butchers because to break the neck correctly requires precision, skill, and follow-through, thereby eliminating any suffering to the animal.

Check for signs of insensibility:
- The chicken's body should be limp and lifeless.
- Eyelids should be limp with no eye movement.
- No vocalization of the bird, and no response to poking the chicken.

Removing the feathers:
- Heat a large vessel with water to approximately 140°F. Do not allow the water to boil or the chicken will cook. If the water is not hot enough, the feathers will not loosen.

- When the water is at the correct temperature, dunk the chicken into the water for about 30 seconds and remove.
- The feathers should be loose enough to easily remove by hand. If not, repeat the procedure above.

Gutting and removal:

- After the chicken has been de-feathered, use a sharp kitchen or butcher's knife to remove the head (if not removed already).
- Begin eviscerating at the cloaca by cutting around the opening of the cloaca and tie the end of the intestines to prevent any feces from expelling as you pull. Gently pull out the guts, using your fingers and knife to carefully separate the membranes attaching them to the body cavity.
- Remove the organs, which should be easy to do by hand. You may need to scrape the lungs off the rib cage.
- Remove the oil gland and sac at the base of the tail.

- Remove the crop, the small, hard part of the esophagus above the gizzard.
- Remove the chicken's feet by cutting them at the knees.

Getting started and positioning the chicken:

- Breaking down a whole chicken into individual cuts is easy.
- First, you'll need a stable surface to cut on, such as a butcher block or a cutting board with moist towel laid flat underneath, and a sharp knife with a slim point. A deboning knife is ideal—it's designed to cut around bones and through joints—but any knife with a thin tip will work. Be sure to thoroughly clean your cutting surface, your knife, and your hands.
- Pat the chicken dry with paper towels. Place the chicken on its back so the breasts are facing up and the drumsticks are against the cutting board and the ends are facing you. Make sure any remaining feathers have been removed from the skin.

Removing the legs:

- Holding the end of one of the drumsticks, take your knife and slice the skin between the drumstick and the breast, running parallel with the lower portion of the breast and along the inner leg until you reach the hip socket.

- Using your hands, press the leg outward while holding the breast—like you're opening a book. The leg should easily break at the hip; you will hear a crack and see the ball and joint hip socket exposed.

- Take the tip of the knife to cut between the ball and socket through the remaining cartilage and muscle into the back portion until the whole leg can be removed.

- Set the leg and thigh aside and repeat on the other side, rotating the bird if necessary. The legs can be kept whole or separated into a drum and a thigh by cutting the white portion of the joint at a 45-degree angle.

Removing the wings:

- Lay the bird on its side and rotate so one of the wings is facing you. Grabbing where the tip of the wing meets the wingette, lift the wing and, using the tip of your knife, cut into the pit of the wing where it connects to the breast. Try to keep the tip of the knife shallow so as not to gouge the breast. Keep going until you until you cut the tendon that keeps the wing attached, then run the knife around the socket joint to remove the wing completely. Repeat on the other side.

- Once removed, the wing can be kept whole or cut into sections. The wing has three sections: the drummette is closest to the breast, the wingette is the middle section, and the tip is the farthest from the bird. These sections can be easily separated by cutting in the middle of the white portion of the joints between each of these sections. The tips contain no meat and can be used to make stock or broth.

Removing the breasts:

- Return the bird to its original position on the cutting board—on its back with the breasts facing up and where the legs were closest to you.

- Hold the bird by the bottom portion of the breast and lift slightly so you can see down the cavity. Locate the ribs, then with the knife running parallel with the cutting surface, cut through the ribs in between the back and under the breast. Both rib portions can be cut simultaneously, or they can be cut one side at a time, depending on the size of your knife. Continue cutting through the neck area until the carcass and ribs are separated from the breasts. If you'd like, save the carcass to make broth or stock.

- Now, you'll have two bone-in breasts that can be left whole or separated. To separate, lay the breast skin-side up, and with one hand on top of the other, press the center of the breast into the cutting surface until you hear a crack and feel the breast flatten. This breaks the ribs attached to the sternum that keep the two breasts together. Cut between the cracked ribs and sternum to separate the two halves into single bone-in breasts.

- To debone the breasts, place the breast skin-side up and lay your palm and fingers flat on the top. Starting with the thick side of the breast, cut parallel to the cutting surface as close to the bones as possible until the ribs can be removed.

- Congratulations—you have now successfully broken down a whole chicken. Practice makes perfect, so be patient, and your skills will improve each and every time.

Butchering Quail & Other Game Birds

Whole, skin-on:

- Butchering quail is really no different than butchering a chicken or other culinary bird, as explained above, except the quail is much smaller and typically involves using kitchen shears instead of a sharp kitchen knife.
- In summary, you can cut the wings off a quail with shears at the joint where they meet the body. You can also use the shears to remove the head and the legs below the drumsticks where there isn't any skin.
- Starting from the neck, cut down both sides of the backbone. Pull the backbone out and the innards will come out with it. Scrape out any remaining innards with your fingers. The heart and liver can be retained for use in a quick sauté or paté.
- Rinse the quail inside and out with clean water.
- Briefly dip the quail in a bowl of organic acid rinse, if desired.
- Place quail in a ziplock bag then into a cooler until ready to use.

Breasted and quartered quail, skin off:

- Hold the quail breast-side up. Pinch the skin on both sides of the keel bone (ridge at the center of the breast) and pull the skin away. It will split and peel away from the breast easily.
- At the tip of the breast near the sternum, push through the abdominal membrane with your thumb and lift the breast to pull it away from the body cavity.
- Locate where the wings meet the breast and

cut through the wishbone with shears on both sides. The breast can now be pulled free.
- Cut the feet away at the bottom of the drumstick. Use the pinch-and-pull technique to remove the skin from the legs.
- Remove the leg quarter, drumstick, and thigh, by cutting along the backbone through the hip joint.
- Briefly dip the quail in a bowl of organic acid rinse, if desired.
- Place breasts and legs in a ziplock bag then into a cooler until ready to use.

Aging Game Birds

Aging game birds has a long history that developed through experience. Pick an image of a medieval castle kitchen and you will find game birds hanging somewhere in the background. The purpose of aging game birds, like other meats, is to allow enzymes to tenderize the meat and develop flavor. It is amazing the difference a few days of aging can make on the quality of game bird meat.

Birds cleaned in the field often benefit from a more thorough second cleaning after returning home. Rinse the birds well in clean water while rubbing with your fingers to remove any blood and feathers. Also pick out any birdshot that can be reached. Dip the birds into an organic acid rinse again, then place into a clean ziplock bag. The birds can now be aged for up to ten days in the refrigerator. After aging, the meat should be cooked immediately or frozen. Each breast lobe can be pulled away from the bone by running your thumb underneath it. A bag of boneless breasts will freeze better than bone-in breasts.

Poultry:
Recipes & Wine Pairings

The following chicken recipes are graciously provided by Petaluma Poultry.

Petaluma Poultry provides locally raised, fresh organic and free-range chicken with ranches in and around Sonoma County, California. As a pioneer in free-range and organic poultry, Petaluma Poultry is dedicated to sustainable farming practices that renew natural resources. Their goal is to produce the finest free-range and organic poultry products while reducing waste, preserving the environment, supporting their employees, and contributing to their local communities.

Recipes for turkey, duck, and pheasant are graciously provided by author James O. Fraioli and Chef John Ash from their James Beard award–winning cookbook, *Culinary Birds.* Quail recipes are graciously provided by Broken Arrow Ranch (see page 205).

Accompanying each recipe are suggested wine pairings provided by J. Lohr Vineyards & Wines and Grgich Hills Estate.

J. Lohr Vineyards & Wines was founded more than four decades ago by Jerry Lohr and is still family owned and operated today. J. Lohr crafts a full line of internationally recognized wines from 4,000 acres of certified sustainable estate vineyards in Monterey County's Arroyo Seco and Santa Lucia Highlands appellations, Paso Robles, and Saint Helena in the Napa Valley. Offering an expressive range of styles, J. Lohr produces five tiers of award-winning releases: J. Lohr Estates, J. Lohr Vineyard Series, J. Lohr Cuvée Series, J. Lohr *Gesture,* and J. Lohr Signature Cabernet Sauvignon.

Grgich Hills Estate is committed to natural wine growing and sustainability. The winery farms their five estate vineyards without artificial fertilizers, pesticides, or herbicides, relies on wild yeast fermentation, and uses passion and the art of winemaking to handcraft food-friendly, balanced, and elegant wines. In keeping with their goal of sustainability, the winery switched to solar power and, beginning with their 2003 vintage, all Grgich Hills wines are labeled "Estate Grown." This guarantees a consistently superior level of quality and it means that Grgich Hills will always remain a shining symbol of prestige and good taste. As founder Miljenko "Mike" Grgich often says, "From our vineyard to your glass, naturally!"

BEFORE WE BEGIN . . . PREHEATING THE OUTDOOR GRILL

There are many options when it comes to selecting an outdoor grill, whether it be wood-burning, charcoal, or gas. In fact, no two grills are alike, yet the foundation is the same. It is important to bring your grill up to the proper temperature before starting the cooking process.

Before igniting your grill, carefully review the manufacturer recommendations on the types of fuel needed. Gas grills are easy, as there's not much to preheating other than turning on the gas, igniting the sparker, and allowing the temperature gauge to reach proper temperature.

Wood-burning, charcoal, and other solid fuel–burning grills can be a bit trickier, as there are additional factors to consider, such as ambient temperature, moisture, the quality of the grill's metal shell, and often, the lack of a built-in thermometer.

For most charcoal grills, select a bag of regular, self-lighting, Kingsford briquettes. This avoids the use of lighter fluid. Stack a pile of briquettes, about 4 or 5 inches high, that covers about half the grill area. Light the charcoal with a flame, and allow the fire to burn out, uncovered, until you are left with embers or the briquettes ashed over. At this point, cover the grill with the lid for 10 minutes, then your grill will be preheated and ready for use.

Whichever grill you are using, make sure you are always operating the grill in a well-ventilated area (always outdoors, never indoors) and away from anything that has the potential to catch fire from a rogue spark.

Bourbon Bacon Wings with Sticky Maple & Crisp Bacon

Serves 4

2 pounds chicken wings

8 ounces applewood-smoked
   bacon, diced (reserving
   1 tablespoon of the bacon fat
   for the Sticky Maple Sauce)

Sticky Maple Sauce (recipe
   follows)

Sticky Maple Sauce

½ cup chicken stock

½ cup brown sugar

½ cup pure maple syrup

¼ cup cold-brew coffee

2 tablespoons bourbon

½ teaspoon salt

½ teaspoon cracked black
   pepper

1 tablespoon bacon fat

Prepare an outdoor grill for direct, medium-high heat; instructions on previous page.

When the grill is hot, add the wings. Grill, turning the wings to get perfect grill marks on both sides while they start to crisp, about 8 to 10 minutes. Internal temperature of the wings should reach 170°F.

Place the bacon in a medium saucepan over medium heat. Cook until crispy, stirring occasionally to cook evenly. Once the bacon is crisp, remove the bacon and strain the drippings from the pan. Reserve at room temperature.

To make the Sticky Maple Sauce, in a medium saucepan over medium heat, combine the chicken stock, brown sugar, and maple syrup. Stir occasionally until reduced by half (Note: the color should darken and take about 10 minutes). Add the coffee and bourbon and return to a boil. Boil for about 3 minutes and add the salt and pepper. Whisk in the bacon fat. Toss the cooked wings in the sauce along with the crisp bacon, arrange on a platter, and serve.

WINE SUGGESTION:

2016 J. Lohr Estates South Ridge Syrah

Varietal aromas of black cherry, blueberry, anise, and black tea are lifted by barrel aging on lees in a 60/40 blend of American and French oak barrels. A touch of floral Viognier and white pepper on the palate, with baking spice on the finish. This wine pairs well with grilled chicken and poultry as well as a slow-roasted pork shoulder and herbed potatoes. For simple, casual fare, try a classic BLT or chicken sandwich.

Braised Chicken Thighs with Artichokes & Edamame

Serves 4

4 large chicken thighs, skin on

Salt and cracked black pepper, to season

1 ounce canola oil

6 baby artichokes, halved, cleaned, and blanched for 3 minutes

4 shallots, peeled and halved

1 cup edamame

2 garlic cloves, peeled and chopped

Olive oil, as needed

½ lemon, juiced

1 tablespoon chopped fresh oregano

1 tablespoon chopped fresh Italian flat-leaf parsley

Preheat the oven to 425°F.

Preheat a heavy-duty skillet (like cast iron) over medium-high heat on the stove. Pat the chicken thighs dry, and season with salt and pepper. Once pan is hot, add the canola oil, followed by the chicken thighs (skin-side down). Brown the thighs, about 5 to 6 minutes, remove from pan, and set aside.

In a large bowl, add the artichokes, shallots, edamame, garlic, and a drizzle of olive oil, and season with salt and pepper. Toss well and spread out on a large baking sheet. Place the browned thighs over the vegetables, and place in the oven. Roast for 13 to 15 minutes, or until the vegetables are browned and the chicken is fully cooked.

To serve, combine the lemon juice with the oregano and parsley. Mix well and drizzle over the chicken and vegetables just before plating.

WINE SUGGESTION:

2017 J. Lohr Estates Falcon's Perch Pinor Noir

When Cynthia Lohr saw a falcon perched next to their Pinot Noir vines, this silky and enticing wine immediately had its name. Enjoy flavors of wild strawberry and sage with bittersweet chocolate on the finish. A pinch of red pepper really sets off this Pinot Noir. It's delicious when paired with Spanish chorizo, paella, or this braised chicken dish. Also matches quite well with mushroom dishes and Pacific salmon.

Chimichurri Marinated Chicken

Serves 4

2 tablespoons fresh oregano, chopped

2 cups fresh cilantro, chopped

5 garlic cloves, peeled and chopped

½ cup olive oil

¼ cup red wine vinegar

1 teaspoon kosher salt

½ teaspoon red pepper flakes

2 chicken breasts (½ per serving), skin on

4 legs (drumsticks)

For the chimichurri, add the oregano, cilantro, garlic, olive oil, vinegar, salt, and red pepper flakes to a blender or food processor. Blend until combined, but still is a little chunky. Place the chicken in a large resealable plastic bag with ½ to 1 cup of the chimichurri. Seal the bag and move the chicken around until all the pieces are coated. Refrigerate for 1 hour, or up to 12 hours.

Preheat a grill to medium heat (page 17).

Arrange the marinated chicken on the hot grill, breasts skin-side down, and sprinkle with a little kosher salt. Cook until the skin becomes dark brown, about 8 to 10 minutes. Note: If you are not used to grilling chicken with the skin on, keep a close watch. The skin will cause flare-ups and lead to burning. Always keep the grill cover down. This helps to maintain a consistent temperature while reducing the cooking time.

Turn the chicken over with tongs, sprinkle with a little more kosher salt, and continue to cook for another 8 to 10 minutes. You want to achieve the same color as before. Turn over again and check the internal temperature of the chicken with a meat thermometer. The chicken is ready when the internal temperature reaches 165°F. If chicken hasn't reached 165°F, continue turning over so you don't burn the skin until the chicken is finished cooking.

Remove from heat and plate.

WINE SUGGESTION:

2016 J. Lohr Estates Arroyo Vista Chardonnay

This savory Chardonnay features lemon cream, brioche, white peach, baked pear, and citrus aromas with floral notes. Rich, silky and Burgundian in style, the J. Lohr Estates Arroyo Vista Chardonnay pairs exceptionally well with this recipe along with herb chicken with toasted hazelnuts, seared scallops with lemon tarragon, or triple crème Brie cheese.

Chicken Provençal with Broccoli Rabe

Serves 4

3 tablespoons olive oil, divided

4–6 boneless, skinless chicken breast fillets

Kosher salt, as needed

Cracked black pepper, as needed

2 tablespoons peeled and chopped shallots, divided

4 garlic cloves, peeled and chopped, divided

¾ cup white wine

1½ cups diced tomatoes, with juice

1 teaspoon chopped fresh rosemary

1 teaspoon fresh thyme

½ cup Kalamata olives, pitted

½ teaspoon capers

1½ pounds broccoli rabe

1 tablespoon lemon zest

Preheat the oven to 350°F.

In a large frying pan, heat 2 tablespoons of olive oil over medium-high heat. Season the chicken with some salt and pepper. When the oil just starts to smoke, place the chicken, skin-side down, in the pan. Cook the chicken until browned on all sides, turning once, about 8 to 10 minutes. Remove the chicken from pan, place on a baking sheet, and place in the oven while you make the sauce.

In the same frying pan used for the chicken, reduce the heat to medium-low. Add half of the shallots and half of the garlic. Keep stirring until the shallots soften, making sure not to brown the shallots or garlic. Add the wine to deglaze the pan and simmer until reduced by half. Add the tomatoes, rosemary, thyme, olives, and capers. Simmer for about 5 minutes, then season with salt and pepper. Reduce heat to low, add the chicken (with juices accumulated while in the oven), cover, and simmer for 5 to 10 additional minutes. Make sure the chicken is cooked through. The internal temperature should be 165°F to 170°F. Place one piece of chicken on each plate. Spoon the sauce over chicken.

In a large pot with lid, bring 4 to 6 quarts of water to a boil. Add a little salt and the broccoli rabe and blanch for 30 to 45 seconds. Drain the broccoli rabe into a colander. Run under cold water until cooled or place in an ice bath to stop the cooking process.

Continued on next page

Preheat a large sauté pan with the remaining 1 tablespoon of olive oil over medium heat. Add the broccoli rabe and the remaining shallots and garlic. Toss to keep the leaves from wilting while making sure not to brown the shallots or garlic. Add the lemon zest and toss. Season with salt and pepper. Plate with the chicken and serve.

WINE SUGGESTION:

2017 J. Lohr Estates Riverstone Chardonnay

J. Lohr's Riverstone Chardonnay is named after their Riverstone Chardonnay vineyards, which have abundant "Riverstones," also called "Greenfield Potatoes," which limit soil depth from one to four feet and provide ideal drainage for the vines. Experience a fresh, youthful texture with flavors of white peach, floral, citrus, baking spices, and honey. This wine can be enjoyed with a variety of dishes, including classic herb-roasted chicken, citrus-marinated halibut, and *moules marinière*.

Citrus-Marinated Chicken Thighs

Serves 4

1 bunch scallions, thinly sliced, divided

½ bunch fresh cilantro

2 garlic cloves, peeled and chopped

1 teaspoon lime zest

1 teaspoon orange zest

¼ cup fresh lime juice

¼ cup fresh orange juice

¼ cup soy sauce

2 tablespoons olive oil

1 tablespoon kosher salt

2 pounds boneless, skinless chicken thighs

Skewers, for grilling

1 lime, wedged and reserved for grilling

In a blender or food processor, add all but ¼ cup of the scallions along with the cilantro, garlic, lime zest, orange zest, lime juice, orange juice, soy sauce, olive oil, and salt. Puree until smooth. Reserve ¼ cup of the marinade.

Place the chicken in a large resealable plastic bag with the remaining marinade. Seal the bag and move the chicken around until all the pieces are coated. Refrigerate for at least 30 minutes. Note: If using wooden skewers, soak the skewers in water while the chicken is marinating.

Preheat a grill to medium heat (page 17).

Remove the chicken from the refrigerator and skewer each piece of chicken with 2 skewers. Place the skewers evenly across the hot grill. After 3 minutes, turn each skewer 90 degrees. After another 3 minutes, flip the skewers over. Turn 90 degrees after 3 minutes, then after another 3 minutes while checking the temperature. Once the internal temperature of the chicken thighs registers 165°F on a meat thermometer, remove the chicken from the heat, cover, and let rest for several minutes. While the chicken is resting, arrange the lime wedges on the grill. Flip after about a minute, then remove from grill after another minute. Serve the chicken with the grilled lime wedges along with the reserved scallions and marinade.

WINE SUGGESTION:

2017 J. Lohr Estates October Night Chardonnay

The 2017 J. Lohr Estates October Night Chardonnay is pale yellow in color, with exotic floral aromas of gardenia, tangerine, baked pear, honeysuckle, and baking spices. Traditional Burgundian winemaking techniques, such as weekly stirring of the lees in French oak barrels, were used to complement these aromatics, providing a creamy palate texture. This wine is perfect with citrus-marinated chicken, eggs Benedict, crab cakes, cedar-plank salmon, and almond-crusted halibut.

Honey Sriracha Drumsticks

Serves 4

2 pounds chicken legs
   (drumsticks)
1 ounce vegetable oil
Salt and cracked black pepper,
   to season
4 tablespoons honey
3 tablespoons sriracha hot
   sauce
1–2 tablespoons chili paste
   (sambal oelek)
2 teaspoons fresh lime juice
1 tablespoon fresh cilantro,
   chopped

Preheat a grill on medium heat (page 17).

In a large bowl, toss the raw drumsticks with the vegetable oil and some salt and pepper. Spread the drumsticks out evenly across the hot grill. Turn them every 2 to 3 minutes to ensure the drumsticks cook evenly and do not burn. The drumsticks should take 17 to 20 minutes depending on their size and temperature of the grill. To ensure the drumsticks are fully cooked, insert an instant-read thermometer into the thickest part of the meat alongside the bone. Bone-in chicken should be cooked to 175°F to ensure the meat is cooked through.

In a separate bowl, combine the honey, sriracha, chili paste, lime juice, and cilantro. Mix well and toss with the fully cooked drumsticks.

WINE SUGGESTION:

2017 J. Lohr Estates Bay Mist White Riesling

This wine takes its name from the mist and fog off Monterey Bay that helped to create a touch of botrytis or "noble rot" in J. Lohr's early Rieslings. Experience aromas of paperwhites, pear, lychee, and lemongrass, complemented by bright acidity, textured palate, and a long finish. Enjoy this wine as an aperitif with ripened goat cheese (Morbier), this delicious chicken drumsticks recipe, spicy ahi tuna sushi, or with wild and flavorful Indian or Thai curry dishes.

Grilled Chicken with Heirloom Tomato & Peach Salad

Serves 4

1 cup balsamic vinegar

1 garlic clove, peeled and minced

1 bay leaf

1 tablespoon honey

4 boneless, skinless chicken breasts

Extra-virgin olive oil, as needed

Kosher salt and cracked black pepper, as needed

2 peaches, quartered and pitted

1 cup heirloom cherry tomatoes, halved

16 basil leaves, torn

½ cup burrata cheese

In a heavy-bottomed saucepan, combine the vinegar, garlic, bay leaf, and honey. Stir with a wooden spoon until the honey has dissolved. Bring to a simmer over medium heat, then lower heat to medium-low and continue to simmer, stirring occasionally, until the reduction becomes syrupy and coats the back of a spoon, about 12 to 15 minutes. Watch closely so the reduction doesn't burn. Keep warm enough to pour until needed. Note: Don't walk away from the reduction while on the stove or you could end up with a burned taste that is not appealing. In addition, make sure to remove the bay leaf before serving.

Preheat the grill for medium heat (page 17).

Brush the chicken breasts evenly with some olive oil and season with kosher salt and cracked black pepper. Place the chicken breasts evenly over the hot grill. Every 3 minutes turn each breast 90 degrees, and turn when needed. Once the chicken breast reaches an internal temperature of 165°F, the chicken is fully cooked. Place the chicken on a cutting board and let rest 5 minutes.

While the chicken is resting, brush the peaches with a little olive oil. Place the peaches, cut-side down, on the grill. Grill for a total of 3 minutes, turning to achieve grill marks on all cut sides. Remove from the grill and let cool to room temperature. Note: When choosing peaches, try to find firm and fragrant peaches, with emphasis on the fragrance.

Continued on next page

On each plate place one chicken breast, then the grilled peaches, tomatoes, basil leaves, and burrata cheese, divided evenly. Season lightly with kosher salt and cracked black pepper. Drizzle 1 or 2 tablespoons of the balsamic reduction over salad just before serving.

Slow-Cooker Chicken Pozole Verde

Serves 4

4 cups chicken stock (see next page)

1 cup water

2 bay leaves

1 pound boneless, skinless chicken breasts, split

15 tomatillos (about 1 pound), husked and cleaned

2 poblano chilies, halved and seeded

2 jalapeño chilies, halved and seeded

1 large yellow onion, peeled and cut into 8 wedges

6 garlic cloves, peeled and mashed

½ cup fresh cilantro, chopped, plus more for serving

1 teaspoon chipotle chili powder

1 teaspoon Mexican oregano

1 tablespoon cumin

Salt

2 (15-ounce) cans hominy, drained

2 tablespoons fresh lime juice

Cracked black pepper

In a large Dutch oven or heavy 12-quart saucepan over medium-high heat, bring the chicken stock, water, and bay leaves to a boil. With tongs, carefully add the breasts. Cover and lower the heat to simmer over low heat until the chicken is cooked through, about 15 to 20 minutes. The chicken is cooked through when a thermometer inserted in the thickest part of the chicken registers 165°F.

Transfer the chicken to a plate and shred. Keep the chicken stock on the burner and turn the heat down to warm. While the chicken is simmering, preheat the broiler. Spread out the tomatillos, chilies, onion, and garlic on a baking sheet. Broil until the tomatillos are blistered, about 5 to 8 minutes.

Remove the vegetables from the oven and place in a food processor/blender. Add the cilantro, chili powder, oregano, and cumin. Puree until smooth, then season to taste with salt. Add the tomatillo puree (scraping out everything) and hominy to the chicken stock in the Dutch oven and stir to combine. Turn the heat up to medium and bring to a simmer, then add the shredded chicken and lime juice. Simmer for 5 minutes more, then taste and season with salt and pepper. Serve in deep bowls with accompaniments such as shredded cabbage, diced avocado, sliced radish, chopped cilantro, lime wedges, and crumbled tortilla chips.

WINE SUGGESTION:

2017 J. Lohr Estates Riverstone Chardonnay

J. Lohr's Riverstone Chardonnay is named after their Riverstone Chardonnay vineyards, which have abundant "Riverstones," also called "Greenfield Potatoes," which limit soil depth from one to four feet and provide ideal drainage for the vines. Experience a fresh, youthful texture with flavors of white peach, floral, citrus, baking spices, and honey. This wine can be enjoyed with a variety of dishes, including classic herb-roasted chicken, citrus-marinated halibut, and *moules marinière*.

SPICY CHICKEN STOCK
Serves 3

1 whole chicken

1 large yellow onion, cut into 2-inch wedges

3 carrots with tops, scrubbed and cut into 1-inch lengths

3 celery stalks with leaves, scrubbed and cut into 1-inch lengths

1 head garlic, cut in half crosswise

1 bunch Italian flat-leaf parsley

4 green serrano chilies, cut in half lengthwise

6 dried chilies de arbol

4 dried Anaheim chilies (California)

1 stalk lemongrass, cut into ½-inch lengths (tough outer layers removed)

1 piece ginger, peeled (about 3 inches)

4 bay leaves

2 tablespoons dried coriander seeds

Cold water, as needed

In a large stockpot, add the whole chicken first. Then add the onion, carrots, celery, garlic, parsley, all of the chilies, lemongrass, ginger, bay leaves, and coriander. Lastly, add the cold water, just enough to cover all of the ingredients. Over medium-high heat and uncovered, bring to a boil, then reduce the heat to a slow simmer. As the stock simmers, skim the foam from the surface, allowing to simmer for a minimum of 30 minutes but not more than 45 minutes.

Carefully remove the chicken from the stockpot and let rest on a rimmed baking sheet. Continue to simmer the stock for another 30 to 45 minutes. Strain the stock through cheesecloth or a fine-mesh sieve into a large bowl or pot. Press on the solids to make sure you get all the flavor and juices. Discard the solids and cool the stock in the refrigerator. When completely cooled, skim the fat off the top that has solidified. Strain again to remove any bits left behind from skimming. Portion the stock for the fridge or freezer. If frozen, the stock will be good for up to 3 months. When the chicken has cooled enough to touch, remove the skin and shred the meat, setting aside for soup or other uses.

Spicy Grilled Chicken with Lemon

Serves 4

2 tablespoons Spanish
  hot smoked paprika

2 tablespoons kosher salt

2 tablespoons cracked
  black pepper

1 tablespoon crushed red
  pepper flakes

1 teaspoon garlic powder

1 teaspoon onion powder

1 bone-in chicken breast,
  skin on, split

4 Meyer lemons, cut in
  half

2 romaine hearts, cut in
  half lengthwise, leaving
  the root intact

Prepare a grill for medium-high heat (page 17). Note: For a gas grill, leave one or two burners off. For a charcoal grill, arrange the ashed-over coals to one side of the grill for indirect cooking.

In a bowl, combine the paprika, salt, black pepper, red pepper flakes, garlic powder, and onion powder. Spoon the seasoning onto each breast, rubbing it evenly into the skin.

Over direct heat, grill the chicken skin-side up for 5 to 8 minutes, or until browned. Rotate the chicken occasionally and moving to the cooler side of grill to control flare-ups. Turn the chicken, skin-side down, rotating occasionally, until browned, about 8 to 10 minutes. Again, watch for flare-ups and move to the cooler side as needed. When brown, not black, move the chicken to the indirect heat side of the grill, skin-side up. Lower the lid and continue grilling and rotating occasionally. Check the temperature with an instant-read meat thermometer inserted into the thickest part of the breast, making sure the thermometer is not touching any bone. The chicken is ready when the internal temperature reaches 165°F, about 20 to 30 minutes. Transfer to a platter and let rest 5 to 10 minutes.

Over direct heat, grill the lemons and romaine, cut-side down, until lightly charred. Remove from the heat and arrange on a platter with the chicken. Squeeze 2 or 3 grilled lemon halves over the chicken and romaine. Serve with the remaining lemons.

WINE SUGGESTION:

2018 J. Lohr Estates Flume Crossing Sauvignon Blanc

Jerry Lohr named this wine for the cement flumes built in 1905 by Clark Colony members to carry the waters of Reliz Creek over the top of the irrigation canals adjacent to the winery's Sauvignon Blanc vines. A crisp, well-balanced Sauvignon Blanc, this exquisite varietal boasts a lively acidity, key lime, grapefruit, and sweet herbs, with a nice textured finish. Enjoy with this savory recipe, or as an aperitif with goat cheese and oysters. Also pairs well with an entrée of sushi or seared scallops with green goddess dressing.

Rachael Sandwich

Serves 1

A Reuben, as you probably know, is corned beef on grilled rye with sauerkraut and Swiss cheese. Though corned beef is traditional, it's nice to change it up with this version using turkey breast.

¼ cup mayonnaise

¼ cup sour cream

2 tablespoons ketchup

2 tablespoons prepared chili sauce, such as Heinz

1 tablespoon Worcestershire sauce

2 teaspoons lemon juice

1 tablespoon horseradish

Kosher salt or sea salt and freshly ground black pepper

2 slices rye, whole-grain, or pumpernickel bread

1 tablespoon Russian dressing or Thousand Island dressing

⅓ pound sliced roasted turkey

¼ cup coleslaw or drained and rinsed sauerkraut

2 slices Swiss cheese

2 tablespoons softened butter or olive oil

To make the Russian dressing (about ¾ cup), in a bowl combine the mayonnaise, sour cream, ketchup, chili sauce, Worcestershire sauce, lemon juice, and horseradish. Season with salt and pepper. Set aside.

Assemble the sandwich by spreading one side of each bread slice with the dressing. Layer the turkey, coleslaw, and cheese on one of the dressed sides. Cover with the remaining bread slice, dressing-side down. Spread top bread slice evenly with half the softened butter. Heat a skillet over moderate heat and place the sandwich buttered side down in the skillet. Spread up-facing side with remaining butter. Cover; grill slowly on each side until golden brown. Serve hot or at room temperature.

WINE SUGGESTION:

Grgich Hills Estate Miljenko's Selection Chardonnay, Napa Valley

The maritime climate of the vineyards where these grapes are grown allows them to slowly ripen and develop complex flavors while maintaining a pleasing natural acidity that is impossible to achieve in warmer areas. This aromatic Chardonnay has a bouquet of refreshing citrus, Meyer lemon, and jasmine. The lively acidity provides a foundation for the rich flavors of crisp Golden Delicious apple and soft white nectarine.

Turkey Tortilla Soup

Serves 6

This is a rendition of the famous soup of the Southwest. The recipe calls for turkey legs, but you could use the whole legs of any bird. The pork, meanwhile, adds deeper flavor to the soup stock.

2½ pounds bone-in turkey legs and/or thighs

1 pound meaty pork bones, such as spareribs or fresh hocks

1 large onion, peeled and quartered

1 head garlic, halved across the equator (don't peel)

1 tablespoon Mexican oregano

⅓ cup vegetable oil

4 corn tortillas

2 tablespoons chopped canned chipotle chilies in adobo, or to taste

⅔ cup chopped fresh cilantro, divided

Kosher salt or sea salt and freshly ground black pepper

2 medium avocados, peeled, pitted, and cut in large dice

6 ounces melting cheese (such as shredded mozzarella, Oaxaca, or Jack)

Lime wedges for serving

Put the turkey, pork bones, onion, garlic, and oregano in a large soup pot. Add water to cover (about 12 cups) and bring to a boil over high heat. Reduce the heat to low and simmer, partially covered, and cook until the turkey is very tender, about 1 hour. Be sure to skim the surface of the stock occasionally of the scum that will rise to the top. Remove the turkey and pork from the stock and place on a cutting board. When cool enough to handle, shred the turkey using your fingers, discarding the skin and bones. If there is any meat on the pork, do the same. Strain the stock, discarding the solids, and set aside.

Meanwhile, put the vegetable oil in a large skillet over medium heat. When the oil is hot but not smoking, fry 2 of the tortillas (one at a time if necessary), turning once, until crisp and golden, 2 to 3 minutes per tortilla. Drain on paper towels. Cut the 2 remaining tortillas into thin strips and add them to the hot oil, stirring to separate them until they are crisp and golden, 3 minutes or so. Drain on paper towels and lightly salt while they are still warm. Set aside.

Add 2 cups of the reserved stock to a blender with the chipotles and ⅓ cup of the cilantro. Crumble the 2 whole fried tortillas, add to the blender, and puree until the mixture is smooth, adding more stock, if necessary.

Continued on next page

Pour the puree and remaining stock back into the pot and bring to a simmer and cook for a few minutes. Add salt and pepper to taste. Stir in the shredded turkey. Divide the avocados, cheese, and remaining ⅓ cup of cilantro among six bowls. Ladle the soup into the bowls and garnish with the fried tortilla strips. Serve immediately with lime wedges to squeeze over.

WINE SUGGESTION:

Grgich Hills Estate Chardonnay, Napa Valley

Grgich's estate Napa Valley Chardonnay is the quintessential representation of Miljenko "Mike" Grgich in a glass. The wine exudes a lively bouquet of freshly squeezed citrus and delicate floral notes. The palate reveals rich flavors of Fuji apple with a hint of pear and stone fruit, progressing seamlessly to a long, elegant finish.

Turkey Picadillo Tacos

Serves 6

Picadillo *roughly translates to "mincemeat" in Spanish. Picadillo is traditionally made with beef or pork, but it can also be made with turkey. Usually made with tomatoes and served with rice, it's also delicious as a filling for tacos, savory pastries such as empanadas, or even as an appetizer served with chips and guacamole.*

4 tablespoons olive oil, divided
1½ pounds ground dark meat turkey
1 large onion, chopped
3 garlic cloves, finely minced
1 large poblano chili, cut in ¼-inch dice (about 1½ cups)
1 tablespoon ancho chili powder
2 teaspoons ground cumin
1 teaspoon ground cinnamon
¼ teaspoon ground cloves
½ cup red wine, plus additional as needed
1 (15-ounce) can diced tomatoes
½ cup golden raisins, plumped in hot water and drained
10 pitted green olives, slivered (about ¼ cup)
Salt and freshly ground black pepper, to taste
12 flour or corn tortillas

Heat 2 tablespoons of the olive oil in a large skillet. Add the ground turkey and brown over high heat. Set aside. Heat the remaining olive oil in the skillet and add the onion, garlic, and poblano and cook for 10 minutes, stirring occasionally, over moderate heat.

Return the turkey and its juices to the pan along with the ancho chili powder, cumin, cinnamon, cloves, wine, tomatoes, raisins, and olives. Reduce the heat and simmer, uncovered, for about 15 minutes. If too dry, add a little red wine, a bit at a time. Season to taste with salt and pepper.

Spoon warm picadillo into fresh corn tortillas and top with any or all accompaniments, such as cilantro sprigs, shredded cabbage, sliced radishes, lime wedges, sliced avocados, queso fresco or crema.

WINE SUGGESTION:

Grgich Hills Estate Rosé, Napa Valley

Grgich's Rosé was crafted in the traditional saignée method, allowing free-run juice to drain from the tank after one to five hours of skin contact. Aromas of watermelon, papaya, and red currants balance the crisp and refreshing flavors of this dry, full-bodied rosé. Serve slightly chilled; it's the perfect pairing for any spicy cuisine.

Spice-Rubbed Grilled Turkey Tenderloins

Serves 4

This is a perfect recipe for warm weather. Try it with a delicious salad like a summer succotash salad.

2 tablespoons brown sugar
1 teaspoon salt
1 teaspoon ground cumin
Pinch cayenne pepper
⅛ teaspoon ground ginger
⅛ teaspoon ground coriander
1½ pounds turkey tenderloin
2 tablespoons olive oil

Combine the brown sugar, salt, cumin, cayenne, ginger, and coriander, and mix well. Brush the turkey tenderloin with olive oil and rub with the brown sugar mixture.

Prepare a grill to 350°F to 400°F (medium-high heat). When it is hot, place the turkey on the grill, cover with the lid, and cook for 8 minutes on each side or until a meat thermometer inserted into the thickest portion registers 165°F. Let it stand at least 5 minutes before slicing and serving.

WINE SUGGESTION:

Grgich Hills Estate Miljenko's Selection Essence Sauvignon Blanc, Napa Valley
Only the best blocks of Grgich's Sauvignon Blanc are used to make this limited-production wine. The wine is fermented in large French oak casks at low temperatures to retain the grapes' delicate aromas. This Sauvignon Blanc has complex aromas and flavors of lemon verbena, peach, and a hint of French vanilla—with a long, mineral-driven finish.

Pesto-Stuffed Turkey Breast

Serves 8 to 10

You could use a traditional pesto mixture or the pistachio pesto suggested here. Some finely chopped and sautéed mushrooms would also make a nice addition. Note: If you have time, chill the prepared breast overnight before cooking.

1½ cups packed fresh basil leaves

⅔ cup chopped unsalted and lightly toasted pistachios

⅓–½ cup extra-virgin olive oil

1 tablespoon poached or toasted garlic

3 tablespoons freshly grated Parmesan cheese

2 tablespoons chopped fresh mint

Zest and juice of 1 small lemon

Kosher salt or sea salt and freshly ground pepper, as needed, to taste

1 (4- to 5-pound) skin-on, boneless turkey breast

Olive oil

⅓ cup finely chopped parsley

2 tablespoons finely chopped poached garlic

3 tablespoons finely grated lemon zest

¼ pound (1 stick) unsalted butter, melted

To make the pistachio pesto, blanch the basil in boiling salted water for 3 seconds, drain immediately, and plunge into cold water to stop the cooking and preserve the green color. With your hands, squeeze as much of the water as you can from the basil. Chop it roughly and add to a blender or food processor with the pistachios, olive oil, garlic, Parmesan, mint, and lemon zest and juice. Puree, scraping down the sides, about 2 minutes. The mixture should be thick, so use a minimum amount of olive oil. Season to taste with salt and pepper.

For the turkey, arrange the turkey skin-side down on a cutting board. Remove the tenderloins and reserve for another use. Make a lengthwise cut about ¾-inch deep down the middle of each breast. Be careful not to cut all the way through. Cover the breasts with plastic wrap. Using the smooth side of a meat mallet or the bottom of a heavy skillet, gently pound the breasts evenly to 1½-inch thickness. Season lightly with salt and pepper and smear the pesto over the breasts, leaving a 1-inch border around the edges.

Starting with one long side of the breast, tightly roll into a cylinder with the skin facing out. Tie the breast at 1-inch intervals with kitchen twine, and then tie the length of the breast with twine to secure it. The objective here is to have a breast that is a uniform log shape so that it will cook evenly. Rub the exterior of the breast

Continued on next page

with olive oil and season with salt and pepper. Combine the parsley, garlic, and lemon zest and sprinkle evenly over the breast. Wrap the breast in plastic wrap and chill for at least an hour and preferably overnight.

Preheat the oven to 375°F.

Unwrap the turkey and discard plastic. Line a rimmed baking sheet with foil and set a rack inside the baking sheet. Place the turkey on the rack and bake, basting the turkey with the butter and turning every 20 minutes or so. Cook until the thickest part of the turkey registers 145°F, about 1 to 1¼ hours. Increase heat to 500°F and continue cooking, turning once, until the turkey is nicely browned, about 10 minutes more. Transfer the turkey to a serving platter and let rest for at least 15 minutes, tented loosely with foil. Remove the twine and slice the turkey crosswise into ½-inch slices to serve.

WINE SUGGESTION:

Grgich Hills Estate Fumé Blanc, Napa Valley

The maritime climate of the vineyards where these grapes are grown allows them to slowly ripen and develop complex flavors while maintaining a lively acidity that is impossible to achieve in warmer areas. On the nose, the wine displays fresh, tropical notes of pineapple, kiwi, and peach—followed by melon, lime, and fresh apple on the palate.

Duck Sausage or Crépinettes

Makes about 20 meatballs

French in origin, a crépinette is a small, slightly flattened sausage made of minced meat, sometimes including truffle, wrapped in caul fat instead of stuffed into a casing. Caul fat is very delicate lacy fat that surrounds the internal organs of four-footed animals. It's worth seeking out, but chances are you aren't going to find it in stock in supermarkets. So here we're making the sausage into meatballs. Flavors here are Moorish Spanish. Serve as an appetizer with a romesco sauce or with pasta and your favorite tomato-based sauce.

1 pound ground duck
¼ cup blanched slivered almonds, lightly
    toasted and chopped
¼ cup golden raisins, chopped
2 teaspoons finely chopped garlic
⅓ cup freshly grated Parmigiano-Reggiano
¼ cup bread crumbs, such as panko
1 teaspoon ground cumin
¼ teaspoon ground allspice
1 teaspoon salt
1 teaspoon smoked paprika
2 teaspoons dried crumbled mint
1 large egg, mixed with a fork
Olive oil for sautéing

In a large mixing bowl, combine the duck, almonds, raisins, garlic, cheese, bread crumbs, cumin, allspice, salt, paprika, mint, and egg wash. With wet hands, form the mixture into rounded 2-tablespoon–size balls. Heat about ¼ inch of the olive oil in a large, nonstick sauté pan over moderate heat. Fry the meatballs until they are browned on all sides, about 8 minutes. Serve immediately or simmer in sauce for a few minutes.

WINE SUGGESTION:

Grgich Hills Estate Merlot, Napa Valley

This Merlot is crafted from grapes grown in Grgich's cooler maritime climate vineyards of American Canyon and Carneros and the warmer Yountville vineyard. Blending the Merlot from all three vineyards creates a rich, robust wine with bright fruit and fresh acidity. This robust Merlot will delight even Cabernet Sauvignon lovers. Its supple, rich texture is graceful with inviting notes of plums, cherries, mixed berries, and a subtle undertone of violets.

Braised Pheasant

Serves 2 to 4

¼ cup extra-virgin olive oil

1 (2½-pound) pheasant, cut into 6 serving pieces

Salt and freshly ground black pepper

1 large white onion, chopped (about 3 cups)

4 large garlic cloves, peeled and slivered (about 2 tablespoons)

2 ounces pancetta, finely diced

1 teaspoon dried oregano

3 whole cloves

2 bay leaves

2 tablespoons tomato paste

1¼ cups dry white wine

3 cups chicken stock

2 tablespoons freshly grated Parmesan cheese

2 tablespoons finely chopped parsley

Heat the oil in a large skillet over moderate heat. Add the pheasant pieces, season with salt and pepper to taste, and brown lightly on all sides, about 5 minutes total. Remove and set aside. To the same skillet, add the onion, garlic, pancetta, oregano, cloves, and bay leaves and cook until the onion just begins to brown, about 5 minutes. Remove excess fat, if desired, and discard.

Return the pheasant to the skillet and stir in the tomato paste, wine, and chicken stock and bring to a boil. Reduce the heat and simmer, partially covered, until the pheasant breasts are tender, 12 to 14 minutes. Remove the breasts and set aside. Continue cooking the leg and thigh pieces for an additional 20 minutes or until tender. Remove the whole leg (thigh and drumstick) and set aside.

Increase the heat to high and boil until the liquid in the skillet has reduced to 1 cup, about 8 minutes. Strain the sauce through a medium-mesh strainer and return to the pan. Season to taste with salt and pepper. Return the cooked pheasant pieces to the sauce to heat through. Mix the Parmesan and parsley in a small bowl. Serve topped with cheese and parsley mixture. This rustic preparation is wonderful with egg noodles, polenta, or risotto.

WINE SUGGESTION:

Grgich Hills Estate Miljenko's Selection Petite Sirah, Calistoga

The grapes for this wine were grown at Miljenko's Vineyard, a thirty-four-acre parcel of land north of Calistoga overlooked by Miljenko "Mike" Grgich's home. This 100% Petite Sirah's pure, dense flavors of ripe blueberry, blackberry, and roasted coffee continue to become more complex in the glass.

Warm Duck Breast Salad

Serves 8

4 Pekin duck breast halves

1 tablespoon olive oil

2 teaspoons minced garlic

2 tablespoons minced scallion

2 tablespoons oyster sauce

2 tablespoons soy sauce, divided

2 tablespoons rice wine or dry
   sherry

2 teaspoons sugar

½ teaspoon 5-spice powder

1 tablespoon roasted garlic,
   mashed

½ cup toasted hazelnut oil

3 tablespoons balsamic vinegar

1 tablespoon fresh lemon juice

1 tablespoon minced chives

1 teaspoon honey, or to taste

Salt and freshly ground pepper,
   to taste

½ cup toasted and skinned
   hazelnuts, cut in rough halves

6 cups gently packed mixed baby
   spicy greens (such as cress,
   arugula, mizuna, tatsoi)

Trim the breasts of excess fat and score the skin side of the breast in a diamond pattern with the point of a sharp knife—through the fat but not into the meat.

In a bowl, make marinade by combining the olive oil, garlic, scallion, oyster sauce, 1 tablespoon of the soy sauce, rice wine (or dry sherry), sugar, and the 5-spice powder. Mix well and coat the duck breasts thoroughly. Allow to marinate at least 2 hours, refrigerated, turning occasionally.

In a separate bowl, make the salad dressing by combining the roasted garlic, hazelnut oil, vinegar, lemon juice, chives, remaining soy sauce, honey, salt and pepper. Mix well and let stand for at least 1 hour before serving for the flavors to develop.

In a heavy skillet over moderately high heat, cook the duck breasts, skin-side down, to brown and render the fat, about 4 minutes. Turn over and cook for another 3 to 4 minutes. Be careful not to overcook. Place the breasts on a cutting board and allow to rest while you compose the salad. Artfully arrange a mixture of baby greens on 4 plates. Add the hazelnuts to the dressing and spoon over the greens. Thinly slice the breasts on the diagonal and arrange on the greens. Serve immediately while the breast is still warm.

WINE SUGGESTION:

Grgich Hills Estate Paris Tasting Commemorative Chardonnay, Napa Valley

For this wine we select only the best grapes, primarily from Grgich's oldest block of Chardonnay, the Old Wente clone planted in 1989. The wine is endowed with the perfect balance of fruity, floral, and mineral components, as well as a seamless structure and texture that is both firm yet transparent and subtle. Intense aromas of ripe pear, apple, apricot, and lemon curd immediately engage your senses, followed by ethereal floral notes of orange blossom and jasmine.

Roast Pheasant Stuffed with Wild Rice

Serves 2 to 4

2 tablespoons butter

1 medium onion, peeled and finely chopped (about 1½ cups)

1 celery stalk, finely chopped (about ½ cup)

2 medium garlic cloves, peeled and finely chopped (about 1 tablespoon)

Kosher salt or sea salt and freshly ground black pepper

1 ounce dried porcini mushrooms, softened in warm water for 30 minutes and chopped

¾ cup sliced mushrooms

¼ cup dry white wine

⅓ cup chicken broth

½ cup golden raisins

1½ cups cooked wild rice

¼ cup chopped flat-leaf parsley

1 tablespoon chopped fresh thyme (1 teaspoon dried)

1 (2½-pound or so) whole pheasant

Preheat the oven to 425°F.

Heat the butter in a heavy skillet over medium heat. Add the onion, celery, and garlic, season lightly with salt and pepper, and cook, stirring frequently, until the onion just begins to brown, about 5 minutes. Add the mushrooms and cook until their liquid has evaporated, about 5 minutes. Add the wine and chicken broth and stir to scrape up any browned bits on the bottom of the pan. Cook until most of the wine and broth have evaporated, about 8 minutes. Transfer to a bowl and stir in the raisins, wild rice, parsley, and thyme and season to taste with salt and pepper; set aside.

Season the pheasant inside and out with salt and pepper. Loosely stuff the pheasant with the rice mixture, then arrange on a rack in a roasting pan. Roast for 10 minutes; reduce heat to 350°F, and roast for 40 minutes or until the juices in the thigh run clear when it is pierced with a knife. Let the pheasant rest for 5 minutes before carving.

WINE SUGGESTION:

Grgich Hills Estate Miljenko's Selection Cabernet Sauvignon, Rutherford

These grapes were grown at Austin's Vineyard, home to Grgich's winery in the heart of Rutherford's viticultural area, one of the world's preeminent sites for Cabernet Sauvignon. This 100% Cabernet Sauvignon demonstrates the distinctive finesse and bright flavors of the famed "Rutherford Dust." The wine has delightful aromas of black cherry, ripe plum, and red roses that are complemented by hints of cinnamon.

Roast Duck Breasts with Grapefruit

Serves 4

This recipe could also be done with chicken breasts. You could also prepare the meat on the grill rather than roasting. As for grapefruit, suggested favorites are the Texas pinks or reds that come to the market in October through June.

1 tablespoon honey

Juice of 2 grapefruits, divided

½ teaspoon ground allspice or
   juniper berry

4 Pekin duck breast halves

Salt and freshly ground pepper

2 tablespoons balsamic vinegar

2 tablespoons sugar

2 cups rich chicken or duck stock

1 cup plus 1 tablespoon
   grapefruit juice

1 cup heavy cream

Kosher salt or sea salt and
   freshly ground pepper

2 grapefruits, sectioned

1 large bunch watercress,
   preferably Upland Cress, with
   big stems discarded

Preheat the oven to 425°F.

Whisk the honey, 3 tablespoons of the grapefruit juice, and the allspice together in a small bowl. Trim the breasts of excess fat and score the skin in a crosshatch pattern, cutting almost but not quite through to the meat. Brush the breasts with the honey mixture, season with salt and pepper, and set aside for at least 15 minutes.

Heat an ovenproof sauté pan over moderately high heat. Add the duck breasts skin-side down and sear until golden brown, about 4 minutes. Turn the breasts over and place in the oven for 5 to 6 minutes more or until the meat is medium rare. Be careful not to overcook. Remove the pan from the oven and then remove the breasts from the pan to a cutting board and allow to rest for at least 3 minutes. Cover loosely with foil to keep warm.

To make the Grapefruit Sauce, combine the balsamic vinegar and sugar in a saucepan and cook over high heat until the sugar is melted and the mixture is reduced to a syrupy consistency, about 2 minutes. Add the stock and 1 cup of the grapefruit juice and reduce over high heat to ¾ cup or so, about 10 minutes. Whisk in the cream and continue to reduce until sauce is nicely thickened, about 5 minutes.

Continued on next page

Remove from the heat, stir in remaining 1 tablespoon of grapefruit juice, season to your taste with salt and pepper, and keep warm. This can be made an hour ahead and kept warm.

To serve, arrange grapefruit sections and watercress on plates. Thinly slice the duck breasts and arrange on top, spoon warm Grapefruit Sauce around, and serve immediately.

WINE SUGGESTION:

Grgich Hills Estate Zinfandel, Napa Valley

This wine comes from Grgich's thirty-four-acre vineyard in Calistoga—the sole source of their Zinfandel. This gorgeous wine reveals tangy raspberry aromas with subtle notes of underlying black cherry lushness. A hint of strawberry coupled with blackberry lingers gently on the palate.

Hoisin-Glazed Quail

Serves 2 to 3

Quail were originally domesticated 1,000 years ago in East Asia, so there is a nice historic tie to these Asian flavors. This recipe is simple enough for weeknight dinners and elegant enough for a dinner party.

4 whole quail (or semi-boneless or boneless or split breasts)
2 tablespoons olive oil
1 teaspoon salt
1 teaspoon cracked black pepper
3 tablespoons hoisin sauce
1 teaspoon ginger, peeled and grated
1 garlic clove, peeled and minced
1 teaspoon soy sauce
1 teaspoon rice vinegar
½ teaspoon sesame oil
¼ teaspoon red pepper flakes

Preheat an outdoor grill for direct, medium heat (page 17).

Season the quail with the oil, salt, and pepper. Set aside. In a mixing bowl, combine the hoisin sauce, ginger, garlic, soy sauce, vinegar, sesame oil, and red pepper. Mix well to combine. Set aside.

Place the quail (breast-side down) on the prepared outdoor grill (page 17). Grill, covered, 5 to 7 minutes (or over medium heat on a preheated gas grill for 5 to 7 minutes; for the oven, preheat to 350°F and bake on a baking tray for 20 to 25 minutes, turning the quail over halfway through). Turn the quail over and brush or spoon the prepared glaze on each bird. Grill for an additional 5 to 7 minutes. The quail are done when plump and firm to the touch. Serve with additional glaze drizzled over the top or on the side for dipping.

WINE SUGGESTION:

Grgich Hills Estate Cabernet Sauvignon, Napa Valley

This Cabernet comes from a blend of Grgich's vineyards throughout the Napa Valley. It entices the senses with layers of complex flavors that continue to evolve in the glass and on the palate. Aromas of black currants, violets, and plums dance in the glass, creating a new experience with every taste. The wine is artfully crafted, well-balanced, and lingers on the palate with a silky mouthfeel, leaving you craving more.

Grilled Marinated Quail

Serves 5 (2 quail per person)

2 cups white wine vinegar

1 cup vegetable oil

4 tablespoons fresh lemon juice

4 whole lemon rinds

3 garlic cloves, peeled and crushed

2 bay leaves

1 tablespoon soy sauce

1 tablespoon A.1. steak sauce

1 tablespoon vermouth

Cracked black pepper, to taste

10 whole quail (or semi-boneless or boneless or split breasts)

In a mixing bowl, combine the vinegar, oil, lemon juice, lemon rinds, garlic, bay leaves, soy sauce, steak sauce, vermouth, and pepper. Divide the marinade in large food-safe plastic bags, add the quail, and gently toss to coat. Close the bags securely and let marinate in the refrigerator 8 hours or as long as overnight, turning occasionally.

Place the quail (breast-side down) on a prepared outdoor grill over medium, ash-covered coals (page 17). Grill, covered, 5 to 7 minutes (or over medium heat on a preheated gas grill for 5 to 7 minutes; for the oven preheat to 350°F and bake on a baking tray for 20 to 25 minutes, turning the quail over halfway through), basting often. Turn the quail over and baste again. Grill for an additional 5 to 7 minutes. The quail are done when plump and firm to the touch.

WINE SUGGESTION:

Grgich Hills Estate 40th Anniversary Chardonnay, Napa Valley

Grgich celebrated their 40th anniversary with a special bottling of the varietal that made Miljenko "Mike" Grgich famous—Chardonnay! This limited-production, elegant Chardonnay harkens back to earlier styles of Chardonnay by selecting lots that showcase the fresh, bright, juicy flavors of crisp apple and pear, driven by refreshing acidity.

Stuffed Quail with Apple and Wild Boar Sausage

Serves 4

2 cups cubed bread

1 (6-ounce) Italian sausage (or wild boar sausage), removed from casing

1 tablespoon butter

1 cup diced apple (Honeycrisp)

2 tablespoons fresh sage, chopped

1 cup chicken broth, divided

Salt and cracked black pepper, to taste

4 semi-boneless quail

Olive oil, as needed

Preheat an outdoor grill for direct, medium heat (page 17).

Slice the bread into ½-inch cubes and place on a baking tray. Toast the bread in the oven lightly, about 5 to 10 minutes. Set aside.

In a large pan over medium-high heat, cook the sausage until it starts to turn golden brown and crumble, about 10 to 12 minutes. Remove the sausage from the pan and reserve. Drain the fat from the pan until about 1 tablespoon remains. Return the pan to the heat and add the butter, apple, and sage. Sauté about 5 minutes. Deglaze the pan with ¼ cup of chicken broth. Add the toasted bread and sausage. Gently mix the stuffing and add the broth ¼ cup at a time until the bread is moist but not soggy. Season to taste with salt and pepper. Remove from heat and allow the stuffing to cool until it can be handled.

Pat the quail dry with a paper towel. Stuff each quail generously with the stuffing. Lightly coat the outside of the breast with olive oil then season with salt and pepper.

Place the quail (breast-side down) on the prepared outdoor grill. Grill, covered, 6 to 7 minutes (or over medium heat on a preheated gas grill for 6 to 7 minutes; for the oven preheat to 350°F and bake on a baking tray for 20 to 25 minutes, turning the quail over halfway through). Turn the quail over and grill for an additional 5 to 7 minutes. The quail are done when plump and firm to the touch.

WINE SUGGESTION:

Grgich Hills Estate Miljenko's Old Vine Zinfandel, Calistoga

Miljenko "Mike" Grgich's home overlooks Grgich's small vineyard in Calistoga, where the few rows of ancient Zinfandel vines that produce this wine were planted more than a hundred years ago. This full-bodied, aromatic Zinfandel is lavished with aromas of enticing plums, warm sandalwood, and white pepper. The wine's concentrated flavors and smooth tannins make it the perfect partner for savory cuisine.

Butchering Rabbit

Similar to the Chicken & Other Birds chapter, the killing and breaking down of a rabbit is far less complex and time-consuming than butchering lamb, sheep, goats, hogs, beef, and large wild game. Nevertheless, when preparing for the humane, timely, and tidy dispatch of a rabbit, foremost we must plan for the considerations of "set and setting." For example, where on the farm or homestead will the slaughter site be located? Will any people will be helping? And with what available tools?

The professional mobile butcher will possess full knowledge of the vast minutiae of all that can go wrong and will plan for and arrange each job in a manner that leaves the least room for error and provides the greatest opportunity for a successful result. As amateur home butchers, we can pick apart a few of the most important concepts and considerations of the professional butcher, thereby increasing the likelihood of attaining a successful and positive home-kill and butchering experience.

Tools and equipment:
- High-powered pellet gun or bolt gun.
- Solid club (like a fish club), if not using one of the guns above.
- Rabbit wringer (if not using one of the tools/guns above).
- Baling twine.
- Rabbit Cincher (if not using baling twine).
- Stainless hanger (if not using the Rabbit Cincher or baling twine).
- Sharp knife (extremely sharp, short stiff blade, sturdy handle).
- Sharpening rod.
- Pruning snips (optional).

- Bucket for blood and guts.
- Hose/nozzle (for proper rinsing of carcass hair and blood).
- Ice water bucket for ice bath of carcass and any organs (if keeping).
- Boning knife.
- Honing rod for sharpening knife.
- Heavy-duty scissors.
- Bins or bowls for butchered pieces.
- Vacuum sealer and bags.

The Kill:
The number one goal of dispatching your rabbit is a humane kill. There are several different ways to humanely dispatch rabbits, including those raised at home. The best method for you will depend on how many rabbits you're raising and the tools you have access to. If this is a one-time project for you, and you only have a handful of rabbits, then a good high-powered pellet gun will give you an instant and humane kill. If you plan on raising rabbits regularly or semi-regularly, the three best humane kill methods are:
- Blunt force stun behind the ears.
- Cervical dislocation.
- Bolt gun.

Blunt force stun:
This is most effective on smaller fryer-size rabbits and is arguably the most humane.
- Lift the rabbit out of its crate by its hips. As you lift, give a swift strike with the club behind the rabbit's ears. This will instantly render the rabbit unconscious.
- Quickly hang the rabbit then bleed.

Cervical dislocation:

This is most effective for most home rabbit raisers, although some bruising may occur on the rabbit's shoulder blades, discoloring and bruising the meat.

- The rabbit's neck is placed behind the rabbit wringer bar, and with a swift pull off the rabbit's back legs, the rabbit is dispatched quickly and painlessly.
- Quickly hang the rabbit then bleed.

Bolt gun:

This is most effective on smaller rabbits in which their skulls are smaller and not as developed.

- The bolt gun is placed just behind the rabbit's ears. When the trigger is pressed, the bolt releases a metal rod under tension and the rod punctures the rabbit's skull/brain, providing an instant kill.
- While this method is instantaneous, you will want to hold the rabbit firmly to the ground after pulling the trigger because the rabbit will likely respond with strong muscle reflexes.
- Quickly hang the rabbit then bleed.

Check for signs of insensibility:
- The rabbit's head and neck should be loose and floppy.
- Eyes should be open with a blank stare. No eye movement or blinking.
- No vocalization of the rabbit, and no response to poking the animal's nose.

Hanging the rabbit:
- Baling twine: Tying baling twine to a tree with a slipknot is a good option. This gives you a lot of flexibility while processing your rabbit. For first-timers, this is a great option.
- Rabbit Cincher: This device is an excellent way to hang rabbits. It's quick and allows you full rotational freedom while processing. If you have many rabbits to process, this is the option that will give you the most flexibility and the least amount of handling while the rabbit is hanging.
- Stainless hanger: Instead of hanging the tool like the Rabbit Cincher, you drill the stainless hanger into a board or tree, making it more permanent.

Bleeding the rabbit:

Words of Caution: Like processing chicken and other small birds, it's critical that you take knife safety seriously as you will find yourself working with your hands and knife very close to each other. It's critical that you are aware of your knife at all times. There are two general practices to instill into your butchering practice. The first is holding the knife the entire time you're processing. The second is having a table close to you so that you can set the knife down during any tugging or pulling steps of the process.

- Once hanging, take the rabbit by the ears and turn its head to the side. Using a sharp knife, make a slice from the rabbit's neck just below the back of the jaw toward the front of the jaw. This will cut the rabbit's jugular and the rabbit will bleed out quickly.
- Turn the head so the rabbit's nose is facing you. Place your knife into the same area you sliced the neck to bleed the rabbit. With knife pressure force against the neck (get the knife into the neck joint as best you can), pull the knife through and remove the head. If you prefer to have the head on, skip this step and continue with skinning.

Skinning the rabbit:

- With the rabbit's belly facing you (upside down), pinch skin on left thigh away from the muscle, then poke the knife into the skin and slice up toward the ankle/foot.
- With the fur now open from the thigh to the ankle, pinch the fur between your fingers and cut it off at the ankle. Grab the fur that has

been cut near the ankle and pull the fur gently toward the anus. Repeat this on the opposite side. You should now have a hanging rabbit with both leg muscles exposed.

- Turn the rabbit so the tail side is facing you. Place your knife tightly against the rabbit's tail and cut through the tail.
- Turn the rabbit back to the belly facing you. Pull the fur away from the abdomen.

Undressing the carcass:

- Pull the fur down until the pelt is completely off and only hanging by the front paws.
- Take your knife (or pruning snips) and place the blade in the joint of the front paw joint. With downward pressure of the knife into the joint, rock the knife gently through the joint and the paw will pop off.

Eviscerating the carcass:

- At this point the rabbit should now be hanging without fur.
- Pinch the skin of the belly and make a small incision in the center of the belly. Open the small incision and put your pointer and middle finger into the rabbit. Spread these two fingers into an upside-down V shape. Move your fingers down the carcass while using the blade of the knife in between the V shape of your fingers. You're now carefully using one continuous slice motion to open the belly with your fingers as a guide.
- Repeat this process in the opposite direction to open the belly from your original incision

from the belly toward the genitals. At this point the belly is fully opened and anus detached, but anus remains in place.

- Pull the anus down and remove from the carcass.
- Pull the innards out through the neck cavity. Detach the liver (if you want to keep it) and discard all the innards into your waste bucket. If you keep the liver, you need to remove the bile sac.
- Remove the heart and lungs.

Cleaning and drying the carcass:
- Wash out the carcass well with your hose and spray nozzle, then spray out the chest cavity and neck area to remove the blood.
- Remove the rabbit's feet.
- Place the rabbit carcass in ice water for about 10 minutes.
- Drip-dry the carcass in a cool-chilled area for about 2 hours. If the space is not available, place the carcass in a large bowl and refrigerate.
- Place the carcass in vacuum-seal bag, seal, and place in the freezer.

Butchering the rabbit:
There are three main parts to a rabbit: forelegs, hind legs, and loin. The loin can be further broken down into rack, saddle, and bellies.

Forelegs:
- The forelegs of a rabbit are easily separated as they are only connected by muscle tissue. With the rabbit laying on its side, lift the foreleg and feel the joint. Cut along the

natural seam under the foreleg, cutting toward the head. With your hand holding the foreleg, make a smooth cut along the seam until the foreleg is removed. Repeat the process on the other foreleg.

Belly:

- With the rabbit on its back, cut the belly off following along where the belly seam follows along the loin. Once you come to the ribs you have two options. Option 1: Cut down the rib cage and remove the belly at the ribs leaving the rib cage meat. Option 2: Cut to the rib cage and fillet the meat off the rib cage.

Hind legs:

- With the rabbit flat on its back, cut along the inside seam where the hind leg connects to the loin. Grab the hind leg and bend in the opposite direction and pop the ball joint out of the socket. Finish removing the leg by cutting from the top of the hind leg toward the tail end of the loin. Repeat on the other leg.

Loin:

- With the belly, forelegs, and hind legs removed, remove the rib cage. With a pair of heavy-duty scissors, cut along the rib cage where it connects to the loin. Repeat on the other side and remove the rib cage. With the rib cage removed, you can cut the loin into a rack and a saddle. If you cut the loin in half directly behind the removed rib cage, you will now have a rack section and a saddle section.

Rabbit:
Recipes & Wine Pairings

The following rabbit recipes are graciously provided by Chef Raymond Southern.

Raymond Southern is an executive chef who uses the culinary skills he has developed all over the world to create memorable dishes. His accolades include Chef of the Year, Grand Gold, five Gold Medals, and one Silver Medal at the Cayman Islands National Culinary Salon, Top Apprentice by Canadian Federation of Chefs de Cuisine, and an appearance with Team Canada at the World Culinary Exposition in Luxembourg.

Accompanying each recipe are suggested wine pairings provided by King Estate.

King Estate was founded in 1991 on the principles of family, stewardship, and tradition. Sitting upon 1,033 acres at the southern tip of Oregon's Willamette Valley, King Estate is the largest certified Biodynamic vineyard in North America. With a third generation of family making wine on their mountain vineyard estate, King Estate remains family owned and farmed, dedicated to the highest standards in winemaking.

Braised Rabbit Legs with Italian Sausage

Serves 4

1 rabbit, cut into 8 pieces (page 54)

Kosher salt and fresh ground black pepper, as needed

4 mild Italian sausage (casings removed and chopped)

Olive oil, as needed

1 yellow onion, peeled and diced

2 celery stalks, diced

1 fennel bulb, diced

1 can plum tomatoes

5 garlic cloves, peeled and minced

All-purpose flour, for dusting

2 cups dry white wine

1 cup chicken stock

2 tablespoons chopped fresh sage

2 tablespoons chopped fresh oregano

1 tablespoon chopped fresh rosemary

Season the rabbit pieces generously with salt and pepper and set aside.

In a large Dutch oven or cast-iron skillet over medium heat, sauté the Italian sausage until browned evenly. Remove the sausage from the pan, careful to keep any grease left over in the pan. Add a little olive oil to the hot pan and add the onion, celery, fennel, and tomatoes. Sauté the vegetables for about 5 minutes, stirring constantly. Add the garlic for an additional minute. Remove from pan, and set aside.

Add enough olive oil to the pan to completely cover the bottom and return to the heat. Dredge the rabbit pieces in flour and fry in the hot skillet until golden brown on each side (work in batches if needed). Once the rabbit is browned, add all of the wine, and reduce by about half in volume. Return all of the rabbit and vegetables back to the pan, add the chicken stock, sage, oregano, and rosemary, and bring to a simmer. Cook on low heat for 1½ to 2 hours, stirring occasionally. When the rabbit is almost falling off the bone it is done. Add the sausage and any grease that came off the sausage.

Serve the rabbit and sauce over buttered broad noodles and freshly grated Parmesan cheese over the top just before serving, if desired.

WINE SUGGESTION:

King Estate "Bacchus Vineyard" Columbia Valley Cabernet Sauvignon

Bacchus Vineyard is a part of the Sagemoor Group of vineyards, established in Eastern Washington in 1968. As a leading source of old-vine fruit, Bacchus Vineyard fruit is in high demand. Planted in 1972, there are over thirty-five acres of Cabernet Sauvignon on the property. Rich flavors of black currant and dark chocolate coat the palate, with coffee elements emerging toward the long, succulent finish.

Chicken-Fried Rabbit

Serves 4

2 teaspoons baking powder

1 teaspoon baking soda

1 teaspoon black pepper

1 teaspoon salt

1½ cups buttermilk

1 egg

1 tablespoon Tabasco hot sauce

4 rabbit bellies (pound and
tenderize them)

Kosher salt and fresh ground
black pepper, as needed

Vegetable oil, as needed

1 cup all-purpose flour,
seasoned lightly with 1 pinch
of salt, pepper, paprika, and
cayenne pepper

In a bowl, whisk together the baking powder, baking soda, black pepper, salt, buttermilk, egg, and hot sauce. Set aside. This is your Chicken-Fried Rabbit Goo.

Lightly season the rabbit bellies with salt and pepper, then dredge in the seasoned flour mixture, followed by the Chicken-Fried Rabbit Goo. Repeat this process a second time.

Add some vegetable oil to come up to at least 1/4-inch of a cast-iron or heavy skillet and place on a high heat. Once the oil is hot, quickly fry the rabbit bellies, turning once, until golden brown on each side (about 3 minutes per side), and let rest on a paper towel before serving.

Serve the Chicken-Fried Rabbit with coleslaw, country gravy, and mashed potatoes, if desired.

WINE SUGGESTION:

King Estate "Weinbau Vineyard" Columbia Valley Merlot

Located in the Wahluke Slope, sub-AVA of the greater Columbia Valley AVA, Weinbau's south-facing alluvial slope consists of perfectly draining soils. The vineyard experiences moderate temperatures that help elongate hang time with ideal ripening conditions. The Kennewick silt loam soils consistently impart distinct Merlot characteristics like blackberry, cocoa, and ripe plum.

German Rabbit Stew

Serves 4

1 rabbit, cut into serving pieces (page 54)

Kosher salt and fresh ground black pepper

Olive oil, for cooking

2 tablespoons unsalted butter

1 yellow onion, peeled and sliced

2 tablespoons all-purpose flour

2 cups chicken stock

Juice from 1 lemon

White wine, to taste

3 bay leaves, cut in half

½ cup sour cream

2 tablespoons capers (with a little bit of the brine from the jar)

¼ cup fresh lemon juice

Italian flat-leaf parsley, for garnish

Season the rabbit pieces very well with salt and pepper and set aside.

Place a Dutch oven or cast-iron skillet over medium-high heat with enough oil to cover the bottom of the pan. Pat the rabbit pieces dry and brown well on all sides. (Work in batches if the pot is too small.) Remove the rabbit pieces once brown and set aside on towels to drain.

Using the same pan, add the butter then the sliced onion and cook until translucent, about 4 minutes. Sprinkle with flour and stir well. Cook, stirring often, until the flour turns golden brown (about 5 minutes).

Return the rabbit to the pot and add enough chicken stock to cover. Use a wooden spoon to scrape any browned bits off the bottom of the pot. Add the lemon juice, white wine, and bay leaves and bring to a simmer. Cover and cook gently until the rabbit almost falls off the bone, about 1½ to 2 hours.

To serve, remove the bay leaf and then remove the rabbit and plate into 4 equal portions. Top with sour cream, capers, and more lemon juice. Check the sauce for seasoning and spoon equal amounts over each portion. Serve with steamed white rice, if desired, and top with chopped fresh parsley to add earthiness.

WINE SUGGESTION:

King Estate "Domaine" Willamette Valley Pinot Gris

King Estate Domaine wines are made from the highest quality, certified Biodynamic fruit sourced exclusively from their estate vineyard in Oregon's beautiful Willamette Valley. This bottle represents the King family's commitment to sustainable agricultural practices and artisan winemaking methods.

Peruvian Style Rabbit Sliders

Serves 4

1 sweet potato, boiled until tender, peeled and set aside

Vegetable oil, for frying

Salt, as needed

1 small yellow onion, peeled and sliced

Olive oil, as needed

1 teaspoon ground cumin

Kosher salt and fresh ground black pepper, to taste

2–3 cups of leftover roasted rabbit meat, cleaned and chopped

½ cup chicken stock

1 tablespoon (or more) aji amarillo paste (available at Latin markets or online)

Slider buns (such as King's Hawaiian)

Lettuce

Tomato slices

Begin by preparing the sweet potato. Add about 2 inches of vegetable oil in a small pot over high heat. Slice the already cooked and cooled sweet potato. Lightly season with salt and fry in the hot oil until golden brown on both sides. Remove, set on paper towels to drain, and reserve.

For the rabbit: In a large pan sauté the onion in a small amount of olive oil until translucent. Add the cumin and salt and pepper and cook an additional minute. Add the rabbit and cook until just heated through. Add the chicken stock and cook until the mixture holds together well when placed in the slider bun. Just before serving, add the aji amarillo a little at a time until you reach the desired spiciness. Note: You can also add a little aji amarillo to your favorite mayonnaise and spread it on the bun before assembling the burger.

Toast the slider buns and assemble with lettuce, tomato, and the fried sweet potatoes.

WINE SUGGESTION:

King Estate "Weinbau Vineyard" Columbia Valley Cabernet Franc

Located in the Wahluke Slope, sub-AVA of the greater Columbia Valley AVA, Weinbau's south-facing alluvial slope consists of perfectly draining soils. The vineyard experiences moderate temperatures that help elongate hang time with ideal ripening conditions. The microclimate produces a richer, more ripe style of Cabernet Franc. Flavors include plum, anise, and tobacco leaf.

Rabbit and Mushroom Ragout

Serves 6 to 8

Serve this ragout over lightly buttered noodles. This recipe is best with a long broad noodle such as fettucine or pappardelle. And don't forget the freshly grated Parmigiano-Reggiano.

2 whole rabbits (cut into pieces for roasting or braising; page 54)

Kosher salt and fresh ground pepper, as needed

All-purpose flour, as needed

Olive oil, as needed

1 large yellow onion, peeled and diced

3 carrots, peeled and diced

3 celery stalks, diced

1 fennel bulb, diced

12 whole garlic cloves, peeled

4 cups dry red wine

1 (28-ounce) can plum tomatoes

2–3 cups chicken stock

3 sprigs fresh sage

1 sprig fresh rosemary

8 cups total mushrooms (chanterelle and lobster mushrooms), roughly sliced

6 cloves garlic, peeled and minced

Red wine or brandy as needed (about 1 cup)

Generously season the rabbit pieces with salt and pepper, then dredge in flour, shake off the excess, and set aside.

In a large Dutch oven or cast-iron skillet, heat some olive oil over medium-high heat. Add the rabbit pieces to the pan and cook until golden brown, about 2 or 3 minutes per side. Transfer the rabbit to a paper towel–lined sheet pan and set aside.

Using the same pan, reduce the heat a little, and add the onion, carrots, celery, fennel, and garlic. Cook to caramelize, stirring quite often so as not to burn the vegetables, about 30 minutes. Once the vegetables are ready, add the wine and reduce by half. Then add the tomatoes, chicken stock, sage, and rosemary, and bring to a boil.

Add the rabbit to the pan and check for seasoning (should be just slightly under-seasoned). Reduce the heat to simmer, cover, and cook until the rabbit is very tender and falling off the bone, about 1½ to 2 hours.

Remove the rabbit pieces from the sauce and transfer to a plate. Set aside until cool enough to touch. Once cool, tear the meat from the bones and shred into smaller pieces. Discard the bones and return the meat to the sauce.

Heat some olive oil in another pan and sauté the mushrooms for 1 to 2 minutes. Add the chopped garlic, then deglaze the pan with red wine or brandy. Reduce the liquid by half, then add the braised rabbit and bring to a boil. Check for seasonings then serve.

WINE SUGGESTION:

King Estate "Freedom Hill Vineyard" Willamette Valley Pinot Noir

Established in 1982, Freedom Hill Vineyard is located in the foothills of Oregon's Coast Range just south of Dallas, Oregon. The Bellpine ocean floor soils provide a perfect match with their Pacific Northwest growing conditions. Intensely aromatic with ripe black cherry and blueberry flavors, this wine is ready to enjoy, but will also benefit from the patience of cellar aging.

Rabbit Leg Confit

Serves 4

4 tablespoons coarse kosher salt

2 tablespoons sugar

1 tablespoon whole juniper
　　berries

1 tablespoon whole black
　　pepper

4 rabbit legs (for best results
　　use hind legs only)

2 cups olive oil

4 fresh thyme sprigs

4 fresh rosemary sprigs

4 garlic cloves

4 dried bay leaves

3 fennel bulbs, sliced lengthwise

16 cherry tomatoes

Kosher salt and freshly ground
　　black pepper, to taste

In a bowl, combine the salt, sugar, juniper berries, and pepper. Next, place the rabbit in a medium bowl. Sprinkle and rub the seasoning mixture well in the legs. Place in the refrigerator for 6 hours or overnight.

Preheat the oven to 275°F.

Remove the rabbit from the seasoning mixture and rinse well. Dry the rabbit with a towel. Transfer to a small Dutch oven. Add the oil, thyme, rosemary, garlic, and bay leaves. Place in the oven and cook until the rabbit is tender and almost falling off the bone, about 5 to 6 hours. Remove from the oven and let cool for 1 hour in the oil. (Note: If you make this a day ahead, you can refrigerate the rabbit overnight in the oil.)

To heat and serve, remove the rabbit from the oil and wipe off excess. Use a little of the oil in a sauté pan. Preheat the pan and add the legs. Brown the rabbit and fennel for about 1 minute on each side and place in a preheated 350°F oven for 10 minutes. Remove the rabbit from the pan and return the pan with the fennel to the stove on high heat. Add the cherry tomatoes and sauté for 30 seconds to 1 minute. Lightly season with salt and pepper.

Serve with sautéed potatoes and your favorite salad. Reserve a little of the cooking oil to pour on top of the rabbit.

WINE SUGGESTION:

King Estate "Temperance Hill Vineyard" Willamette Valley Pinot Noir

One of the higher-elevation vineyards in the Willamette Valley, the world-renowned Temperance Hill Vineyard has established a reputation for excellence. This sustainably grown vineyard has been carefully cared for by Dai Crisp since 1999, yielding fruit that lends itself to elegant, complex wines. This Pinot Noir is no exception, with earthen notes of blackberry and truffle.

Rabbit Loin "Saltimbocca"

Serves 2

4 boneless rabbit back loins
  (2 per person)
Kosher salt and fresh ground
  black pepper, to taste
Olive oil, as needed
8 large sage leaves
2 long thin slices prosciutto
2 large cloves garlic, peeled and
  minced
1 small shallot clove, peeled and
  minced
2 ounces Marsala wine (or
  slightly sweet red wine)
6 ounces chicken stock
1 tablespoon cold butter

Preheat the oven to 425°F.

Lightly season the rabbit loins with salt and pepper. (Note: Go easy on the salt as the prosciutto is already salty.)

Heat a large sauté pan with olive oil and very quickly (so as not to overcook) sear each side of the rabbit loins. Remove the rabbit and set aside to cool (save the pan). Once cool, stick 4 sage leaves around each loin, and wrap each loin in prosciutto. Reheat the same pan and sear the prosciutto-wrapped loins lightly on each side, then place in the oven for 3 minutes. Remove from the oven, set rabbit loins aside to rest, and return the pan to high heat on the stove top. Add a little more olive oil and the garlic and shallot. Deglaze the pan with Marsala and cook 30 seconds. Add the chicken stock and cook to reduce the liquid by half or to desired consistency. Turn the heat off, check for seasoning, and stir in the cold butter. Slice the rabbit loins into medallions, on the bias, and arrange them on your plate. Pour the sauce over the top. Serve with braised red cabbage and roasted or mashed potatoes, or with pasta noodles of your choice, if desired.

WINE SUGGESTION:

King Estate "Crater View Vineyard & Seven Hills Vineyard" Oregon Grenache-Syrah-Mourvedre

Wines made from the classic grape varietals found in France's Southern Rhône region—Grenache, Syrah and Mourvedre—are often referred to as a "GSM." This varietal combination is typically made from warm growing regions and delivers wines with jammy, dark fruit character and elegant complexity. King Estate hopes you enjoy this Oregon take on GSM, from a world-renowned Walla Walla vineyard, Seven Hills, and Rogue Valley's Crater View Vineyard.

Roasted Rabbit Chili

Serves 4 to 6

Olive oil, as needed

1 medium yellow onion, peeled and chopped

1 medium red bell pepper, seeded and chopped

1 medium green bell pepper seeded and chopped

Kosher salt and fresh ground black pepper, to taste

4 teaspoons ground cumin

4 teaspoons ground chili powder

4 large cloves garlic, peeled and minced

1 (15-ounce) can whole plum tomatoes

1 (7-ounce) can diced green chilies

2 (15-ounce) cans beans of your choice (kidney, pinto)

2 cups chicken stock

2–3 cups leftover roasted rabbit meat, cleaned and chopped

Heat a medium saucepan over medium-high heat and add the olive oil. Add the onion and peppers, and cook until the onion is slightly translucent, about 2 minutes. Add a small amount of salt and pepper and the cumin and chili powder and cook 1 additional minute. (Note: Lower heat as needed so as not to burn.) Add the garlic and cook 1 additional minute. Add the tomatoes and green chilies and cook for 2 to 3 minutes. Add the beans and chicken stock and bring to a boil.

Reduce heat to a simmer and cook for 1 hour. Add the chopped rabbit meat and cook 1 additional hour. Check for additional seasonings, then serve with chopped fresh cilantro, chopped scallions, chopped red onions, sour cream, crispy tortilla chips, and hot sauce of your choice, if desired.

WINE SUGGESTION:

King Estate "Sonrisa Vineyard" Columbia Valley Tempranillo

Sonrisa Vineyard sits at a slightly higher altitude than its surrounding growing regions. Because of this, the vineyard is located in an area that is slightly cooler than many Columbia Valley growing regions. As the principal grape of Rioja, Tempranillo has become known for full-bodied wines, with flavors tending toward blueberry, leather, and clove.

Swedish Rabbit Meatballs

Serves 5 to 6

A quick culinary tip: Take about 1 teaspoon of the uncooked meatball mixture and cook in a hot skillet until done. Taste the meat and adjust the seasonings to your liking. It's always better to do this before making all of the meatballs and finding out after the fact that they are all under- or over-seasoned.

1 pound ground rabbit

1/4 cup fresh bread crumbs

2 tablespoons chopped Italian flat-leaf parsley

1 pinch ground allspice

1 pinch ground nutmeg

1 pinch garlic powder

1 pinch onion powder

Kosher salt and fresh ground black pepper

½ yellow onion, peeled and finely chopped

1 egg

Olive oil, as needed

1 stick butter

½ cup all-purpose flour, or more if needed

2 cups chicken stock

1 cup heavy cream

1 tablespoon Worcestershire sauce

1 teaspoon Dijon mustard

In a medium-sized bowl, combine the ground rabbit, bread crumbs, parsley, allspice, nutmeg, garlic powder, onion powder, salt, pepper, chopped onion, and the egg. Mix together until well combined.

Divide and roll the mixture into 10 large or 20 small meatballs, depending on your preference. Heat a large skillet with olive oil and add the meatballs (in batches if needed) and brown all sides. Set the meatballs aside.

In the same pan, or one large enough to hold all of the meatballs, melt the butter and then add the ½ cup flour and whisk until it turns brown. Slowly stir in the chicken stock, then the heavy cream. Add the Worcestershire sauce and Dijon mustard and bring up to a simmer and let the sauce thicken. Add more flour if the sauce isn't thick, and add salt and pepper to taste. Add the meatballs and simmer for about 5 minutes.

Serve the meatballs over steamed rice or lightly buttered egg noodles. Sprinkle with chopped parsley just before serving.

WINE SUGGESTION:

King Estate "Kennel Vineyard" Willamette Valley Chardonnay

Established in 2007, Kennel is nestled in the Willamette Valley, halfway between Corvallis and Monmouth, Oregon. Consisting of twenty-eight acres, Kennel is considered a warm site, but benefits from coastal breezes and cool nights. This wine was aged in 30 percent new French oak, and underwent malolactic fermentation and sur lie aging. The resulting wine is a silky, full-bodied Chardonnay.

Whole Roasted Rabbit

Serves 2

Juice from one lemon (reserve the lemon halves after juicing)

4 ounces butter, melted

½ cup white wine

1 whole rabbit

Kosher salt and fresh ground black pepper

4 cloves garlic, peeled and finely chopped

3 large sprigs fresh sage, roughly chopped

½ yellow onion, peeled and roughly chopped

Olive oil, as needed

1–2 cups chicken stock

Preheat the oven to 350°F.

In a bowl, combine the lemon juice, melted butter, and wine. Set aside.

Season the rabbit generously (inside and out) with salt and pepper. Stuff the belly with garlic, sage, onion, and the lemon halves. Using your hands, rub the butter and wine mixture all over the inside and outside of the rabbit (reserving some extra mixture for later).

Heat some olive oil in a large Dutch oven or cast-iron skillet over medium-high heat. Place the rabbit in the pan on its side, being careful to keep the stuffing inside the belly. Sear each side to a light brown. Add about a half cup of chicken stock to the pan and a little of the leftover butter-wine mixture, and place in the oven uncovered for 30 minutes.

Gently turn the rabbit to its other side, add a little more of the liquid ingredients, cover loosely with foil, and continue to cook an additional 1 hour. During this time, check the rabbit every 20 minutes and add a little more of the liquid ingredients each time.

Remove the rabbit from the oven and set aside to rest for at least 15 minutes. During this time, place your pan on high heat and add the last of the liquid ingredients and more chicken stock as needed. Turn down to a simmer and reduce the sauce to your desired consistency (feel free to add more stock, wine, lemon, or salt and pepper to adjust to your taste). Season with salt and pepper.

Carve the rabbit into desired pieces and serve warm with the sauce.

WINE SUGGESTION:

King Estate "Domaine" Willamette Valley Pinot Noir

King Estate Domaine Pinot Noir is made from the highest quality, certified Biodynamic fruit sourced exclusively from their estate vineyard in Oregon's beautiful Willamette Valley. This bottle represents the King family's commitment to sustainable agricultural practices and artisanal winemaking methods.

Butchering
Lamb, Sheep & Goat

When preparing for the humane, timely, and tidy dispatch of lamb, sheep, or goat, we must foremost plan for the considerations of "set and setting." For example, where on the farm or homestead will the slaughter site be located? What time of day? How many people will be helping? What tasks will be assigned to which people, and with what available tools?

The professional mobile butcher will possess full knowledge of the vast minutiae of all that can go wrong and will plan for and arrange each job in a manner that leaves the least room for error and provides the greatest opportunity for a successful result. As amateur home butchers, we can pick apart a few of the most important concepts and considerations of the professional butcher, thereby increasing the likelihood of attaining a successful and positive home-kill experience.

Preparation and animal handling:

- Corral the animal(s) and withhold feed for twenty-four hours prior to the planned slaughter date.
- Make sure the animal has continual access to water.
- When *knocking* an animal, having close proximity to the animal is ideal. Experienced slaughtermen will always prefer knocking a calm animal at close range. Great lengths should be taken to ensure the animal is corralled comfortably and is very calm prior to knocking.

Knocking tools:

- There are many makes and models of firearms and captive bolt guns that can successfully "knock" a lamb, sheep, or goat when discharged at the appropriate distance. Always have a backup plan and ideally a loaded backup firearm should the first shot not drop the animal.
- A captive bolt gun is a perfect tool for lamb, sheep, and goats. They are quiet, which is very useful on small farms, urban farms, and in situations where a firearm is not legal or practical. Bolt guns can be held with one hand while the free hand is used to help maneuver the animal into position. Lamb, sheep, and goats are relatively easy to handle, so it is ideal for the slaughterman to be in direct contact with the animal when taking aim to knock.

Additional tools:

- Knives: lamb skinner knife used for skinning, jointing, and gutting. A 5- to 6-inch boning knife used for trimming.
- Halter (optional) for walking the animal to the knocking site and/or for controlling the animal's head position during knocking.
- Carabiner (optional) and California hook connected to a waist belt to fix the foreleg into position during foreleg skinning.
- Butcher's twine for tying weasand (esophagus).
- Hoist, winch, or tractor for lifting the carcass.
- Two plywood 4x4s (or any other implement) for cradling the carcass into position on the ground.

- Gambrel and strap, chain, or rope for hoisting from hind legs.
- Thin wire for hoisting from forelegs.
- Water source. Ideally a hose but also a bucket of water.
- Barrel to pelt and put stomach contents in, if needed, to remove from the slaughter site.
- A vinegar solution spray of 2.5 percent vinegar to water (optional) for cleaning purposes.

Slaughter site:

- The ideal slaughter site has mostly to do with convenience, ease of handling, and ensuring calmness of the animal. The slaughtermen may also want to consider the drainage and accessibility of the site. Will the water and blood be able to drain easily from the site? Can a water hose reach the site? If not, can buckets filled with water be used for washing and cleanliness? Can a tractor or truck access the site easily without getting stuck? If power is needed, can an extension cord reach the site?

Knocking tips:

- Lamb, sheep, and goats are relatively easy to handle, so it is ideal for the slaughterman to be in direct contact with the animal when taking aim to knock.
- In some situations, a halter is useful to bring a lamb, sheep, or goat to the exact location where knocking will commence. A halter can be left on during knocking if deemed necessary, and then removed after knocking, prior to bleeding.

- Memorize the position where the brain is located and try to visualize the brain location before approaching the animal. Remember that the brain extends from the spinal cord, so it is useful to look at the animal's neck and draw an imaginary line upward from the line of the spinal cord toward the skull.
- Lamb, sheep, and goat and sheep skull geometry can vary greatly from breed to breed. Do not attempt to take a shot until you have taken a close look at the animal and have a clear idea of where the brain is positioned.
- Having a second person to restrain the lamb, sheep, or goat's body is very useful so that the knocking person can focus on maneuvering the animal's head in preparation for the shot.
- Knocking can occur from any number of positions in front, behind, or to the side of the skull, as long as the bullet is directed toward the brain. Most commonly, lamb, sheep, and goats are knocked from the "poll" area, which is in the back of the skull in proximity to where the horns would be.

Check for signs of insensibility:

- The animal's head and neck should be loose and floppy.
- Eyes should be open with a blank stare. No eye movement or blinking.
- Tongue should hang out limply.
- No vocalization of the animal, and no response to poking the animal's nose.
- The tail should be relaxed and hang limply.

Bleeding lamb, sheep, or goat:

- Position the body in the direction where you would like the blood to flow.
- Extend the head/neck of the animal to tighten the neck skin and put yourself into a position where you will not be kicked as the animal's nervous system may cause it to thrash about.
- Perform a "transverse method" bleed by inserting a boning knife directly behind the hinge of the jaw, close to the spine, and cut outward away from the spine, thereby opening up the neck.
- After opening the neck, turn the knife back around and sever connections close to the atlas joint. Put the knife away and manually hyperextend the head of the animal toward its back, thereby popping open the atlas joint. This popping of the atlas joint will help you later when it is time to remove the head.

Hoist and cradle:

- If the sheep/goat is heavy, hog-tie it and mechanically hoist it into a cradle. If light enough, two people can lift it into the cradle. If not using a cradle, then it can be worked on the ground.

Skin forelegs and remove trotter section:

- Clean/scrape the forelegs and neck with a currycomb and/or a hose if the animal is excessively dirty. These are the areas you will open with the knife, and if these areas are clean and shorn the result will be a cleaner carcass.

- With the animal's back to the ground and legs in the air, insert the lamb skinner knife between the dewclaw of each foreleg, and open the pelt all the way along the inner leg and inner shoulder, ending your cut line alongside the brisket area. Next, which is optional, insert the Cali hook attached to the carabiner at the waistband to hold the foreleg taut while proceeding to skin out each foreleg. Additionally, make a cut line along the midline of the neck toward the head. Skin out each foreleg and each side of the neck during this stage.
- Great care should be taken to not let the dirty exterior of the pelt fold or flop back on the clean carcass during the skinning process.
- Remove the trotter section at the joint.

Hoist and punch pelt:

- Attach thin wire straps to the forelegs and begin hoisting with the use of a winch. Stop hoisting when the animal is at a comfortable height for punching.
- With clean hands and forearms, punch the pelt away from the carcass. Use your thumb and fingers to leave as much "fell" (membrane) and meat on the carcass as possible. After punching, if the carcass has "tiger stripes" all the way along its back, this is a sign that you have accomplished leaving the fell and meat where it belongs on the carcass.

Hoist and peel pelt:

- After punching the pelt clear around the back, front, and sides all the way to the pelvis, drape the pelt inside out over the hind legs.

- Using a wire strap wrapped around the loose hanging pelt, fasten the pelt to a stable point on the floor.
- Hoist the carcass upward and watch as the pelt peels around the hips. Stop winching once the pelt is below the bung.
- Sever the tail and sever the attachments around the bung. Clear the pelt from the hind legs with clean hands or a knife.
- Pull the pelt the remainder of the way down with clean hands. Knee or pull the pelt until it is below the hind shanks.
- Sever the pelt below the hind shanks. Remove the rear hooves at the joint.

Gambrel hind legs and lower foreleg winch to clear weasand:

- Insert the gambrel into the hind legs and affix overhead. The carcass should now be wired by the forelegs and gambreled by the hind legs.
- Lower the foreleg winch to a point where the animal's back is parallel to the ground.
- From this position, the neck will be hanging in such a way that it will be easy to trim the shoulders and open the weasand area.
- Trim the shoulders, if necessary, to remove any hair or dirt that resulted from knifing open the pelt in this area.
- Access the weasand by trimming the meat and fat along the midline of the neck. Expose the esophagus and trachea.
- Separate the esophagus from the trachea and cut off the trachea. With one hand holding the esophagus (weasand), punch

into the cavity with your fingers on the other hand to clear the esophagus. The esophagus should be free of attachments and able to slide easily within the cavity of the neck and thoracic area.

- Tie the esophagus with butcher's twine to prevent the contents of the esophagus from leaking out. Sever the esophagus below the string after tying.

Invert carcass:

- Lower the foreleg winch and remove the wire strap so that the forelegs are free-hanging toward the ground.

- The carcass should be hanging by the hind-leg gambrel.

Split pelvic bone at cartilage:

- Pop open the pelvis cartilage with a boning knife or saw with a handsaw.

Clear bung and gutting:

- Either using your hand or an optional node hook, knife around the bung to clear it from the interior of the pelvis. Once cleared, hold the bung with the non-knife hand, being careful not to spill the contents of the bung onto the clean carcass.

- With either a lamb skinner or boning knife, split open at the midline of the belly with the knife pointed away from the guts and the knife hand wedged between the guts and the belly fascia.
- As the guts spill forth, simultaneously begin guiding the bung tube down toward the ground, severing attachments and connections with your knife. Take care not to puncture the bung tube as you pull it down. Also, take care not to pull the kidney fat or kidneys away from the interior of the carcass.

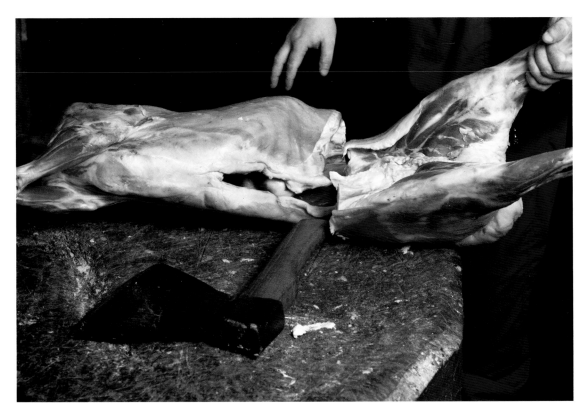

- With the bung tube pulled down and hanging below the forelegs, allow the guts to remain attached near the diaphragm. Locate the liver on the right side and sever the attachment at the liver.
- Put your knife away. Grab the stomach and intestines with one hand and punch down toward the spleen with the other. Everything will be held by the weasand at the point. Grab the weasand (esophagus) and pull it out so that it does not rip due to the force of gravity on the heavy guts.
- After removing the stomach, intestines, and spleen, go back and remove the liver and puncture the membrane of the diaphragm.

- Remove the lungs and heart by knifing very close to the interior of the spine and separating the attachments in the thoracic area to loosen.

Trim, hose, and bacterial intervention:

- Trim any areas of the carcass that may have been smeared with contaminants such as hair, dirt, feces, ingesta, etc.
- Hose with pressurized water.
- Spray down with a vinegar solution cleaning spray of 2.5 percent vinegar to water (optional).

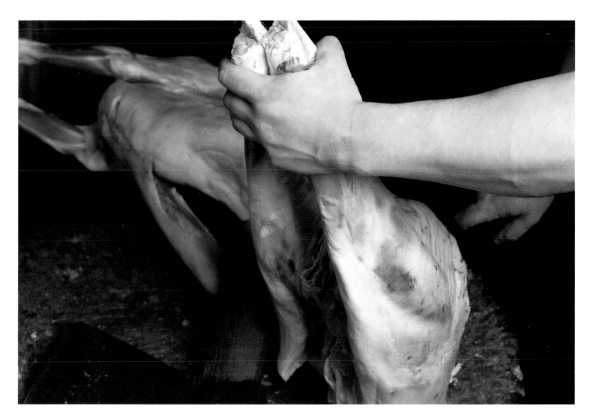

Cooling and aging considerations:

- For optimal aging, bring the carcass down to a temperature below 38°F and above 32°F in as short of an amount of time as possible.
- Allow to age at these temperatures from a hanging position for minimum of 48 hours before fabricating.

Fabricating prep, tools, and considerations:

- One 5- to 6-inch boning knife for boning and trimming.
- One 8- to 12-inch steak knife for cutting steaks and trimming.
- Band saw, handheld saw, or other sawing tool.
- Clean table.

Fabrication methods:

- There are many and varied carcass breaking strategies and techniques, so it doesn't matter whether we break the carcass into primals from a hanging position or on a table.

Decide on breaking point for flank and brisket:

- In many cases the flank sections will be separated from the attachments at the hind leg and a straight cut will be made next

to the saddle, parallel to the spine, and 1 to 3 inches from the lumbar loin muscles (erector spinae).

- In some cases, this straight cut line will be extended across the rib cage to a point along the humerus bone, 2 inches above the elbow joint. The meat will be knifed and the rib bones and humerus will be sawed to create a brisket/navel section attached to the flank section. This outcome will result in a boned and rolled lamb navel.

- In cases where a long lamb breast/navel is not desired, the flank section can be removed at the 13th rib and the brisket can be removed later on in the process.

Decide on removal of tenderloin:

- After the flank removal, in some cases the tenderloin will be removed whole. In other cases, the butt of the tenderloin will be left on the sirloin and the tapered end of the sirloin will be included in the saddle chops (loin chops).

- In other cases, the butt of the tenderloin will be partially peeled from the sirloin and kept attached to the saddle section.

Decide on breaking point for hind legs:

- It is common to separate the hind legs between the last lumbar vertebra and the first sacral vertebra.

- It is common to saw in the middle of the second-to-last lumbar vertebra.
- After breaking the hind legs from the lumbar section, saw along the sacral vertebrae to separate the hind legs.

Hind-leg fabrication:
- Remove the aitchbone and remove the shank at the joint.
- Remove the femur bone to create a boneless lamb leg.
- If desired, straight cut the sirloin from the round at the ball and socket joint area. Straight cut the sirloin against the grain for sirloin steaks.

- Seam the boneless lamb round into smaller boneless roasts: top round, bottom, eye of round, and sirloin tip.

Decide on breaking point for rib rack and saddle:
- It is common to break the rib (thoracic area) from the saddle (lumbar loin area) between the last two ribs.
- Knife between the ribs. Either saw through the middle of a vertebra or find a joint between the vertebrae and knife to pop the joint open. Finish cutting through the meat with a knife.

Decide on saddle (lumbar area) fabrication:

- Debone the vertebrae to produce a tied boneless saddle roast.
- Cut the deboned and tied saddle roast into boneless steaks of the desired thickness.

Decide on thoracic area (rib rack) fabrication:

- Saw the rib rack to the desired rib length. At this point, it may be decided to leave the ribs long for an elegant rib rack aesthetic. In contrast, it may be decided to saw the ribs short to create a shorter rib roast and a rectangular short-rib section.
- It is possible to "chine" the rib rack with a saw, thereby creating a "chined" lamb rack aesthetic.
- Cut between the ribs to produce bone-in lamb rib chops.
- Debone the entire lamb rack to produce a boneless roast or boneless rib steaks.

Decide on breaking point for shoulder:

- Breaking the rib from the loin is commonly done between the 4th and 5th rib or between the 5th and 6th rib.
- Would you like a bigger shoulder and smaller rib rack? Or a larger rib rack and smaller shoulder?
- Knife between the ribs. Either saw through the middle of a vertebra or find a joint between the vertebrae and knife to pop the joint open. Finish cutting through the meat with a knife.

Decide on shoulder fabrication:

- The square cut shoulder commonly will be cut into the bone-in arm and blade chops. Equally common, the shoulder will be deboned and rolled for a boneless roast. It can be daunting for the novice to debone the shoulder because of the irregular shape of the scapula. Proceed with caution.
- To cut the arm chops, begin at the humerus (upper arm) bone. Cut one or two (depending) chops by knifing and sawing perpendicular to the arm bone.
- Flip the remaining shoulder portion and begin cutting the blade chops on the thoracic side of the square cut shoulder. Cut the blade chops to the desired thickness by knifing and sawing parallel to the direction of the rib bones.

Decide on neck fabrication:

- The shoulder will flow into the neck area. The neck can be deboned for a boneless neck roast, used for trim, or portioned into braising chops or bone-in neck roast.

Trim and sausages considerations:

- In many situations, lamb, sheep, or goat trim will be utilized for sausages. It is a good idea to decide on how much or how little sausage, and therefore trim, will be desired.
- The areas of the flanks, shanks, breast, neck, and shoulders are all commonly used for ground sausage when the need for sausage trim is high. When the demand for trim/sausage is not present, all of these areas can be left as roasts, braising cuts, or cubed for stew meat.

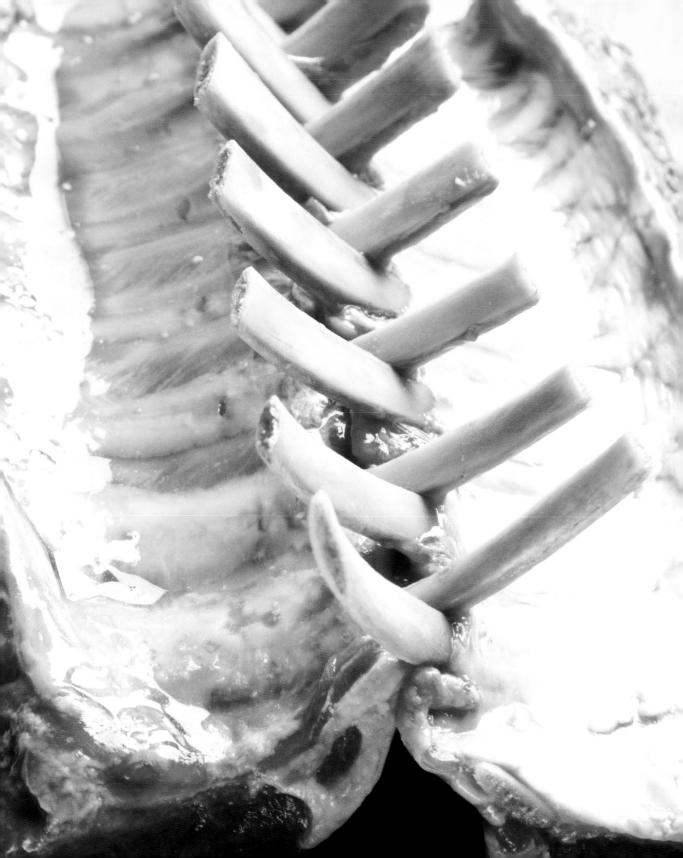

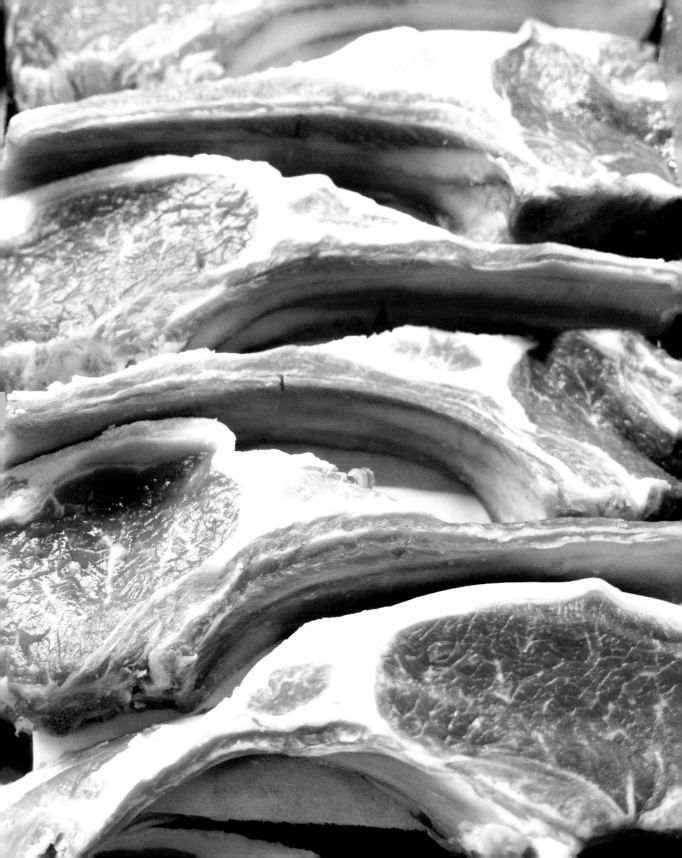

Lamb, Sheep & Goat: Recipes & Wine Pairings

The following recipes are graciously provided by Chef Aaron Tekulve.

Aaron Tekulve is the executive chef and owner of Surrell, a private dining company and pop-up dinner series, and a rising star in the chef and restaurant industry in Seattle, Washington. He also competed on the Food Network TV show *Chopped*. Although he didn't win the $10,000 prize and bragging rights, he demonstrated his strong culinary skills and was viewed as a true professional and great chef. Much of Aaron's culinary experience stems from his time cooking at James Beard Award–winning restaurant Canlis.

Accompanying each recipe are suggested wine pairings provided by Wagner Vineyards Estate Winery.

Wagner Vineyards Estate Winery is one of the oldest and most recognized wineries in the Finger Lakes region of upstate New York. Five generations of the Wagner family have grown grapes in the deep, glacial soils of Seneca Lake. This heritage of grape-growing has provided an intimate connection to the land and a deep passion for the art of winemaking. Today, Wagner is 100 percent estate grown and bottled, cultivates over 215 acres of grapes, produces 30,000 cases of wine, and welcomes over 85,000 visitors per year. Wagner Vineyards has been one of the region's most popular wine-tasting destinations since opening in 1979 and is now celebrating more than forty years of business.

Lamb Belly Pastrami

Serves 4

Lamb belly is a delicious alternative to pork belly, short ribs, and brisket. Lamb belly also performs well in the pastrami-making process.

Brine:

1 gallon water

¾ cup kosher salt

2 teaspoons Himalayan pink salt, optional

⅓ cup white sugar

¼ cup brown sugar

6 large cloves garlic, peeled and smashed

2 tablespoons pickling spice

1 (5-pound) lamb belly, cleaned of excess fat

Braise:

1 yellow onion, peeled and rough chopped

1 large carrot, chopped

Sachet of ¼ cup pickling spice and 2 bay leaves

1 quart chicken stock

Rub:

1 tablespoon black peppercorns, toasted and ground

1 tablespoon coriander seed, toasted and ground

Begin by making the brine. In a large pot, add the water, salt, pink salt (if using), white and brown sugar, garlic, and pickling spice. Bring to simmer, remove from heat, and let cool. Place the lamb belly in a food-safe container and pour enough brine over the lamb until fully submerged. Weigh the belly down with a plate and refrigerate for two days.

Preheat the oven to 350°F.

Remove the lamb belly from the brine and thoroughly rinse off with cold water. Place the belly in a braising pan and add the onion, carrot, and sachet. Cover the belly with chicken stock, then cover the lamb with parchment paper followed by a sheet of aluminum foil. Seal the edges well. Place in the oven and braise for 2 to 3 hours, or until just fork-tender. Remove from the oven, remove the foil lid, and let cool for 1 hour before storing in the refrigerator to further cool for 2 to 3 hours, or overnight.

Prepare an electric/outdoor smoker with hickory chips set at 200°F (instructions follow).

Remove the lamb belly from the braise, scraping away any of the melt fat. In a bowl, combine the peppercorns and coriander, and rub the lamb belly liberally with the spice rub. Place the seasoned lamb belly in the smoker and smoke for 1 hour. Remove the lamb belly from the smoker and slice thinly before serving as a Reuben sandwich or just by the slice with your favorite mustard and pickles.

Preparing and Preheating the Electric Smoker
Even though manufacturers may say you don't need to preheat your electric smoker, it's best to have the unit preheated and operational before you're ready to smoke. This process also helps maintain a consistent temperature environment. For this recipe, we're using the Smokin Tex Pro-Series Stainless Steel Electric Smoker that we have situated on a stable solid foundation. Make sure you also choose a dry, sheltered, and well-ventilated location. Do not expose the smoker to any rain or snow. Prior to plugging the smoker into an outlet, remove the smoking tray and fill three-quarters with dry wood chips (this recipe calls for hickory). Return the tray to the smoker, making sure it is securely in place. Plug the smoker into an outlet and set the knob on the top of the unit to the desired temperature (in this case 200°F). The smoker will be properly preheated when you see a steady stream of white smoke being expelled from the ventilation hole on top of the unit. That's your sign that you're ready to smoke.

Lamb Tartare with Rye

Serves 4

2 tablespoons whole-grain mustard seeds

1 tablespoons Worcestershire sauce

2 tablespoons extra-virgin olive oil

1 teaspoon fish sauce

2 tablespoons shallots, peeled and finely minced

1 teaspoon garlic paste

1 tablespoon ginger paste

2 tablespoons capers, chopped

2 tablespoons fresh basil, finely chopped

12 ounces lamb loin, cleaned

Salt and black pepper, to taste

2 tablespoons red wine vinegar, plus more to taste

Cilantro leaves or micro cilantro, for garnish

Rye crisps, as needed

In a small bowl, combine the mustard, Worcestershire sauce, olive oil, fish sauce, shallots, garlic, ginger, capers, and basil.

Cut the lamb loin into a rough ¼-inch dice or smaller and place in a separate medium-sized bowl. Season with salt and pepper and mix together lightly. Dress the lamb with the mustard mixture and stir together. Season additionally with salt, pepper, and red wine vinegar.

To serve, using a three-inch ring mold, take about a quarter of the lamb tartare and press it into the mold. If you do not have a ring mold, simply place a nice scoop of the tartare on each plate. Garnish with the cilantro leaves and a stack of rye crisps.

WINE SUGGESTION:

Wagner Vineyards Estate Winery, Reserve Pinot Noir, Finger Lakes, New York

This limited-production Pinot Noir is made using handpicked grapes from a single vineyard centrally located on the Wagner farm. This wine is completely fermented on the skins and is aged for a year in a combination of French and American oak.

Roasted Rack of Lamb with Charred Scallion Salsa Verde and Seasoned Greek Yogurt

Serves 4

Cooking oil (grapeseed), as
  needed
2 8-chop racks of lamb
Salt and black pepper, as
  needed
2 sprigs fresh thyme, chopped
1 sprig fresh rosemary, chopped
3 garlic cloves, peeled and
  lightly crushed
3 tablespoons butter
½ cup Charred Scallion Salsa
  Verde (recipe follows)
½ cup Seasoned Greek yogurt
  (recipe follows)

Preheat the oven to 400°F.

Heat a couple tablespoons of oil in a large sauté pan to medium heat. Generously season the lamb racks with salt and pepper. Place one lamb rack, fat-side down, in the pan to slowly render. It is important the fat is well rendered and caramelized, which should take 3 to 4 minutes. Repeat with the other rack, making sure to drain off excess fat if necessary. Next, turn and place both racks, loin-side down, in the pan so the racks are standing upright. Once caramelized, reposition the racks so they create a large "V" in the pan with the opening and the freshly seared loin facing you. Turn the pan down to medium and add the thyme, rosemary, garlic, and butter. Allow the butter to melt while giving the aromatics a chance to infuse their flavor. At this point, begin basting each rack. Continue to baste for 1 to 2 minutes, or until the racks are well basted. Remove the racks from the pan and transfer them to the roasting pan with rack. Pour the butter with aromatics over the racks.

Place the roasting pan with lamb racks in the oven and cook for 10 minutes. Using a cooking thermometer, check the temperature of the lamb. If below 125°F, continue to roast in the oven checking every 5 to 10 minutes. Once the lamb reaches 125°F, remove from the oven and let rest in a warm part of the kitchen for 7 to 10 minutes. During the resting period, the lamb will rise in internal temperature to approximately 135°F. Cut each rack into 4 chops and serve with Charred Scallion Salsa Verde and a dollop of Seasoned Greek Yogurt.

CHARRED SCALLION SALSA VERDE
Makes about ½ cup

To make homemade garlic or ginger paste, use a Microplane and simply zest the garlic or ginger into a bowl. Mash with the back of a spoon and you have fresh paste.

1 bunch scallions
1 teaspoon garlic paste
1 teaspoon ginger paste
1 teaspoon serrano pepper,
    seeded and finely minced
2 tablespoons fresh cilantro,
    rough chopped
1 teaspoon fish sauce
¼ cup extra-virgin olive oil,
    more as needed
2 tablespoons fresh lime juice
Salt and black pepper, to taste

Move the rack in the oven to the top rung and preheat the boiler to high.

Spread the scallions on a sheet tray and place under the broiler. Roast until about one-third of the scallions are blackened. Remove from the oven and let cool. Remove the root end of the scallions, finely chop, and place in a medium bowl. To the scallions, add the garlic and ginger paste, serrano pepper, cilantro, fish sauce, olive oil, lime juice, and salt and pepper to taste. Stir until well combined. Add additional oil if necessary to loosen the mixture. Note: If making in advance, add the lime juice right before serving.

SEASONED GREEK YOGURT
Makes about ½ cup

½ cup Greek yogurt

2 tablespoons extra-virgin olive oil

1 lemon, zest and juice

1 teaspoon garlic paste

Salt and fresh ground black pepper, to taste

In a small bowl, combine the yogurt, olive oil, lemon zest and juice, garlic paste, and salt and pepper to taste. Mix well before serving.

WINE SUGGESTION:

Wagner Vineyards Estate Winery, Meritage, Finger Lakes, New York

Meritage is, by definition, "A wine blended from traditional Bordeaux grape varieties in America." The Wagner Meritage blend is comprised of Merlot, Cabernet Franc, and Cabernet Sauvignon and it is only produced as a result of ideal growing seasons that yield exceptional vinifera. Only five of the last fifteen years have made the cut: 1999, 2001, 2007, 2010, and 2012. Each grape variety was aged separately in American oak barrels of varying age, and the final blend was made from carefully selected individual barrels.

Roasted Leg of Lamb and Summer Vegetable Salad with Cilantro and Feta Cheese

Serves 4

2 pounds leg of lamb, trimmed

Cooking oil (grapeseed), as needed

Salt and black pepper

¼ cup butter

2 sprigs fresh rosemary

2 garlic cloves, peeled

1 cup fresh chanterelle mushrooms

1 cup fresh yellow corn

1 cup halved cherry tomatoes

1 cup green beans, blanched and cut into ½-inch pieces

2 tablespoons peeled and finely minced shallots

1 teaspoon garlic paste

1 bunch fresh cilantro, rough chopped

¼ cup fresh mint, rough chopped

⅓ cup extra-virgin olive oil

2 tablespoons sherry vinegar

½ cup crumbled feta cheese

If possible, the night before cooking season the leg of lamb generously with salt and black pepper.

Preheat the oven to 350°F.

In a large sauté pan over medium-high heat, add enough oil to lightly coat the pan. Add the lamb and sear on all sides. Reduce the heat to medium-low and add the butter, rosemary, and garlic cloves. Baste the lamb for 1 to 2 minutes. Remove the lamb from the pan and transfer to a roasting pan with rack. Pour the infused butter and oil over the lamb. Place the lamb in the oven and roast for 1 hour. Check the temperature of the leg of lamb by inserting a cooking thermometer into the thickest part of the meat. Once the thermometer reaches 130°F, remove the lamb from the oven and let rest. During this time the lamb will rise in temperate to a nice medium-rare.

In a large pan over medium heat, sauté the chanterelles until lightly caramelized. Add the corn and cook for 1 minute, then place in a large bowl along with the mushrooms. To the pan, add the tomatoes, beans, shallots, and garlic paste and season with salt and pepper. In a small bowl, combine the cilantro, mint, olive oil, and sherry vinegar. Pour the warm vinaigrette over the vegetables and mix everything together one last time. Taste and adjust seasoning if necessary.

Slice the lamb against the grain and place on a serving platter; top with the Summer Vegetable Salad and a sprinkle of the crumbled feta cheese over the top.

WINE SUGGESTION:

Wagner Vineyards Estate Winery, Dry Rosé of Cabernet Franc, Finger Lakes, New York

Wagner Vineyards' Dry Rosé is crafted using 100 percent Cabernet Franc grapes, the first Bordeaux variety to make its home in the estate's vineyards. Harvested at midnight, this Rosé achieves its pale pink hue through a 10-12 hour cold-soak prior to press and cool fermentation. This bone-dry Rosé is the perfect way to enjoy a warm summer evening but is versatile enough to find a spot on your dinner table year-round.

Sheep and Pork Meatballs with Pancetta Marinara

Serves 4

1 pound ground sheep

1 pound ground pork

2 tablespoons garlic paste

¼ cup shallots, peeled and
finely minced

2 teaspoons chili flakes

1 teaspoon ground fennel

¼ cup fresh chopped rosemary

2 tablespoons salt

1 tablespoon fresh ground black
pepper

1 cup bread crumbs

2 eggs

1 cup fresh ricotta cheese

2 cups fresh grated Parmesan-
Reggiano cheese, divided

Cooking oil (grapeseed), as
needed

4 cups Pancetta Marinara Sauce
(recipe follows)

In a large bowl, combine the ground sheep and pork. Press the ground meat flat around the bowl and evenly spread the garlic paste, shallots, chili flakes, fennel, rosemary, salt, pepper, and bread crumbs. Gently mix the meat and seasoning together until just incorporated. Add the eggs, ricotta, and 1 cup of the Parmesan-Reggiano cheese. Mix until fully combined. Test some of the meatball mixture by making a small patty and cooking it. Adjust the salt and pepper if necessary.

Preheat the oven to 450°F.

Using an ice cream scooper, portion the meatballs onto a sheet tray. Lightly oil your hands and round each of the freshly scooped meatballs. Lightly oil the meatballs as well. Place the sheet tray with meatballs into the oven. Bake for 10 minutes, or until lightly caramelized.

In a large pot or sauté pan, warm the Pancetta Marinara Sauce over medium heat. Once the meatballs are out of the oven, add them to the sauce and braise for 20 to 30 minutes, or until the meatballs are cooked through. Garnish with the remaining cup of Parmesan-Reggiano cheese just before serving.

PANCETTA MARINARA SAUCE
Makes about 3 cups

2 tablespoons olive oil

1 cup pancetta, cut into ¼-inch dice

1 yellow onion, peeled and finely minced

¼ cup garlic, peeled and finely minced

1 cup red wine (Cabernet Sauvignon)

2 (28-ounce) cans crushed San Marzano tomatoes

2 bay leaves

2 tablespoons butter

Red wine vinegar, to taste

Salt and black pepper, to taste

Preheat a large pot to medium heat. Add the olive oil to coat the bottom of the pot. Then add the pancetta and cook until golden brown. Add the onion and garlic and sweat them until translucent and the onions begin to caramelize. Deglaze the pan with the red wine and reduce by half. Add the tomatoes and bay leaves. Reduce the heat and cook for 1 hour at a very low simmer, stirring every 15 minutes. To finish, remove bay leaves, stir in the butter, and adjust the seasoning and acidity, to taste, with the red wine vinegar, salt, and pepper.

WINE SUGGESTION:

Wagner Vineyards Estate Winery, Merlot, Finger Lakes, New York

An exceptional representation of a cool-climate Merlot, this medium-bodied wine is bursting with aromas of black cherries, plum, and a hint of dark chocolate. A smooth, fruit-driven, and food-friendly wine.

Sheep Ragù with Fettucine and Parmesan-Reggiano

Serves 4

This ragù can be prepared 2 to 3 days ahead. Simply chill uncovered until cool and store in an airtight container in the refrigerator until ready to use.

Cooking oil (grapeseed), as needed

1 pound sheep leg or chuck, ground

8 ounces pork, ground

Salt and black pepper

1 cup chopped carrots

1 cup chopped celery

1 cup peeled and chopped yellow onion

½ cup chopped fennel

3 ounces pancetta, thinly sliced, finely chopped

1 cup red wine (Cabernet Sauvignon or Merlot)

2 (28-ounce) cans San Marzano tomatoes, crushed

1 tablespoon fennel seed, toasted

1 tablespoon crushed chili flakes

2–3 bay leaves

1 pounds fresh-made or store-bought dried fettucine noodles

2 tablespoons butter

2–3 tablespoons red wine vinegar

4 ounces Parmesan-Reggiano, freshly grated

2 tablespoons finely chopped Italian flat-leaf parsley

Heat a large saucepan over medium-high heat. Coat the bottom with a couple tablespoons of cooking oil. When hot, place a thin layer of the ground sheep and pork in the pot and lightly brown. While the meat is cooking, season with salt and pepper while making sure to break the meat apart with a spatula or cooking spoon so the meat has a fine-crumbled texture. As the meat is browned, transfer to a bowl and repeat the process in the same pan until all of the meat is cooked.

Next, place the carrots, celery, onion, and fennel in a food processor and pulse until the vegetables are finely pureed. Add a couple more tablespoons of oil to the pot and add the pancetta and lightly crisp. Then add the vegetable puree and cook for 3 to 4 minutes. Deglaze the pot with the red wine and reduce by half. Once reduced, add the crushed tomatoes, reserved meat, fennel seed, chili flakes, and bay leaves. Stir the mixture together. Cook over medium heat until the sauce begins to simmer. Reduce the heat to low, partially cover the pot to allow for reduction, and cook for 1 to 2 hours, stirring every 20 to 30 minutes. Remove bay leaf before next step.

Bring a large pot of water to boil and season with salt. (Note: Add ¼ cup of salt for every gallon of boiling water.) Cook the pasta according to package directions, or until al dente. In a large sauce pan, heat the ragù over medium-high heat with a few tablespoons of pasta water or chicken stock. Add the cooked pasta, butter, and red wine vinegar, and toss together until fully combined. Divide the pasta equally on warm plates and garnish with the cheese and parsley.

WINE SUGGESTION:

Wagner Vineyards Estate Winery, Unoaked Chardonnay, Finger Lakes, New York

This Chardonnay is 100 percent stainless-steel fermented, allowing the fruit characteristics of the grape to shine. Both fruity and floral on the nose, this Unoaked Chardonnay has a palate full of apples and pears that finishes with a hint of lemongrass and a silky texture. The winemaker uses three different yeasts for complexity during fermentation. This wine is a blend from several different Chardonnay vineyard blocks, including the Dijon clone of the grape.

Sheep Tacos with Cojita Cheese, Spicy Pickled Shallots, and Pepitas

Serves 4

Although the recipe calls for a 4-to-6-pound piece of meat, remember that after cleaning of excess fat, the overall weight will decrease. In addition, when cooking, the shoulder could lose around 30 percent in water weight, so 4- to 6-pounds can turn into as little as 2 pounds of final product. Please consider this when selecting the size of shoulder for this recipe.

1 (4- to 6-pound) boneless sheep shoulder, cleaned and trimmed of fat

Kosher salt and black pepper, to taste

Cooking oil (grapeseed), as needed

1 large yellow onion, peeled and thinly sliced

4 cloves garlic, peeled and thinly sliced

1 cup chicken stock

1 tablespoon ancho chili powder

1 tablespoon ground cumin

1 tablespoon chili powder

2 bay leaves

1 (14½-ounce) can crushed San Marzano tomatoes

Flour or corn tortillas

2 avocados, pitted, peeled and chopped

½ cup Spicy Pickled Shallots (recipe follows)

½ cup pepitas, roasted and salted

1 cup crumbled Cojita cheese

1 cup fresh cilantro, rough chopped, for garnish

Preheat the oven to 350°F.

Clean and remove the excess fat from the sheep shoulder and portion into 3 or 4 large pieces. Season well on all sides with salt and pepper.

Heat a Dutch oven (with lid), or a large heavy-bottomed sauté pan or cast-iron pan, over medium to medium-high heat. Add 2 to 3 tablespoons of cooking oil to the pan and sear the sheep shoulder on all sides. Place the seared shoulder into a glass 9 x 13 or similar-sized dish unless using the Dutch oven. If using the Dutch oven, place the seared sheep shoulder in a bowl after searing and reserve. Reduce the heat of the pan to low and add another tablespoon or two of oil. Add the onion and garlic and sweat. Add the chicken stock, ancho chili, cumin, chili powder, and bay leaves. Mix well and scrape any bits from the bottom of the pan. Add the crushed tomatoes to the chicken stock mixture, bring to a simmer, then pour over the sheep shoulder in the glass 9 x 13 dish or add the shoulder back to the Dutch oven. Tightly wrap with a foil or place the lid to the Dutch oven on top and transfer to the oven.

Braise the sheep shoulder for 2½ to 3 hours, turning the meat every 45 minutes. The meat is done when it is fork-tender and just starts to shred.

Remove the bay leaves and discard. Using tongs or two forks, shred the meat and mix into the sauce in the pan. Note: This can be made 2 to 3 days ahead. Just make sure to store in an airtight container in the refrigerator.

To serve, warm the tortillas by toasting over an open flame or steaming them in a foil pouch. Assemble the tacos starting with the braised sheep shoulder followed by the avocados, Spicy Pickled Shallots, pepitas, Cojita cheese, and cilantro.

SPICY PICKLED SHALLOTS

Makes ½ cup

½ cup peeled and thinly sliced
  shallots
1 garlic clove, peeled and
  smashed
1 serrano pepper, seeded and
  thinly sliced
1 teaspoon kosher salt
½ teaspoon whole cumin seed
½–1 cup white wine vinegar

In an airtight container, add the shallots, garlic, serrano pepper, salt, and cumin, and top with vinegar. Let marinate for 24 hours before serving. Note: Do not expose to heat.

WINE SUGGESTION:

Wagner Vineyards Estate Winery, Fathom 107, Finger Lakes, New York

Wagner Vineyards, located on the eastern shore of Seneca Lake, is situated directly east of the deepest point of the lake. At over 640 feet, or 107 fathoms, deep, this enormous volume of water provides year-round temperature moderation and allows for the preservation of natural acidity. Due to this opportune location, Wagner is able to consistently produce outstanding vintages of Riesling and Gewürztraminer, which comprise this limited-production blend. Both the name of this blend and the label on the bottle are an ode to Seneca Lake and the exceptional growing conditions it provides.

Marinated Goat Chops with Creamy Polenta

Serves 4

2 cups red wine

¼ cup red wine vinegar

¼ cup soy sauce

1 tablespoon fish sauce

1 tablespoon fresh ground black pepper

1 teaspoon chili flakes

4 garlic cloves, peeled and roughly chopped

2 shallots, peeled and roughly chopped

2 bay leaves

4 (8-ounce) goat chops, about 1-inch thick

4 cups beef stock

2–3 tablespoons high-heat cooking oil (grapeseed), as needed

2 tablespoons butter

2 sprigs fresh thyme

2 garlic cloves, peeled and cracked

4 cups creamy polenta, cooked according to package directions

In a food-safe airtight container or plastic bag, add the wine, vinegar, soy sauce, fish sauce, pepper, chili flakes, garlic, shallots, and bay leaves. Shake well and add the goat chops. Let the meat marinate in the refrigerator for 24 hours, turning the bag every 8 hours.

The next day, remove the steaks from the marinade and wipe off all of the marinade. Strain the marinade and reserve for making the sauce.

In a medium sauté pan, add the strained marinade and beef stock. Bring to a simmer and reduce by three quarters or until the liquid fully coats a spoon. Reserve for saucing the steaks.

Preheat the oven to 400°F.

With a large sauté pan over medium-high heat, sear the goat chops in some oil on all sides and finish by adding the butter, thyme, and garlic to the pan. Baste the chops for 1 minute, then transfer them on a rack in a roasting pan and pour the butter and herbs over the steaks. Place in the oven until the internal temperature of the chops is about 125°F to 130°F. Remove from the oven and let rest for 5 to 7 minutes before serving.

To serve, place a scoop of creamy polenta on the plate, rest a chop next to it, and sauce generously.

WINE SUGGESTION:

Wagner Vineyards Estate Winery, Reserve Chardonnay, Finger Lakes, New York

This fruit-forward Chardonnay is initially fermented in stainless steel, then barrel-aged in French oak. This limited-production wine has just a touch of oak, lending to its complexity, silky texture, and full mouthfeel.

Goat Stew

Serves 4

6 pounds boneless goat meat, cut into 1-inch cubes (see page 84)

Kosher salt and fresh cracked black pepper, to season

¼ cup hot smoked paprika

2 tablespoons ground cumin

Cooking oil (grapeseed), as needed

2 tablespoons butter

1 cup peeled and small-diced yellow onions

2 tablespoons peeled and rough chopped garlic

2 cups carrots cut into ½-inch rounds, plus 1 carrot cut in half and greens removed

1 (28-ounce) can crushed San Marzano tomatoes

1 cup red wine (Cabernet Sauvignon)

4 cups beef stock

2 bay leaves

1 cup Yukon potatoes cut into ½-inch cubes

1 tablespoon rough chopped fresh thyme

¼ cup sherry vinegar, plus more to taste

¼ cup chopped Italian flat-leaf parsley, for garnish

Start by thoroughly seasoning the goat meat with the salt, pepper, paprika, and cumin. Meanwhile, preheat a large pot to medium-high heat. Add 2 to 3 tablespoons of oil to the pot and sear all the goat meat while working in batches. Move the seared meat to a bowl and reserve. Turn the pot down to medium-low heat and add the butter and onions and sweat them for 1 minute before adding the garlic and the whole carrot. Continue to sweat the onions, garlic, and carrot, being careful not to caramelize them. Add the crushed tomatoes and cook for 2 to 3 minutes. Deglaze the pan with the red wine and reduce by half. Then add the beef stock, bay leaves, and the reserved goat meat. Bring the mixture to a low simmer and let cook for approximately 1½ to 2 hours, or until the meat is just becoming fork-tender. Add the potatoes and 2 cups of carrot rounds, and cook for another 20 to 30 minutes, or until they are both tender. Finish the stew by adding the thyme, sherry vinegar, and adjusting the seasoning with salt and pepper. Garnish with the fresh chopped parsley.

WINE SUGGESTION:

Wagner Vineyards Estate Winery, Cabernet Franc, Finger Lakes, New York

Cabernet Franc has quickly become one of the premier red vinifera varietals in the Finger Lakes. Since Cabernet Franc is so cool-climate friendly and versatile, in 2017 Wagner Vineyards added to the six and a half acres of Cabernet Franc vines already under cultivation. This very lightly oaked Cabernet Franc is medium bodied with beautiful tannins, notes of ripe blackberries and blueberries, and just a touch of vanilla.

Goat Enchiladas with Ancho Chili Sauce

Serves 4 to 6

4 pounds boneless goat shoulder, cut into a 3 or 4 large pieces

Salt and fresh cracked black pepper, to season

3 dried ancho chilies, stems and seeds removed

1 tablespoon cumin seeds

1 cinnamon stick

½ cup pumpkin seeds

High-heat cooking oil (grapeseed), as needed

1 large yellow onion, peeled and thinly sliced

4 cloves garlic, peeled and thinly sliced

½ cup tequila

½ cup golden raisins

2 quarts chicken stock

16–20 (6-inch) corn tortillas, toasted

2 bay leaves

12 ounces crumbled goat cheese

1 cup fresh cilantro, roughly chopped

Season the goat shoulder well with salt and black pepper on all sides. Preheat a Dutch oven or large straight-sided pot with lid over medium heat. Add the dried ancho chilies and toast them for 3 or 4 minutes. Remove the chilies from the pot and place them in a bowl. Next, add the cumin seeds, cinnamon stick, and pumpkin seeds and toast them lightly and add to the bowl with the chilies. Pour 2 or 3 tablespoons of oil into the pot and add the onion and garlic and sweat them until translucent. Deglaze the pan with tequila and add the raisins, chicken stock, 4 of the tortillas, and the bowl of toasted ingredients. Simmer the ingredients for 30 to 45 minutes, or until everything is softened. Blend the ingredients thoroughly until smooth and pass through a strainer. Reserve the sauce until needed.

Next, add 2 to 3 tablespoons of high-heat cooking oil to the pot and sear the goat shoulder pieces. Pour the ancho chili sauce over the goat, add the bay leaves, and bring to a light simmer. Place the lid on the pot or attach a tight foil lid. Place in the oven and braise for 2½ to 3 hours, or until fork-tender, and you are able to shred the goat. Remove and discard the bay leaves. Reserve 4 cups of the sauce from the braise for building the enchiladas. Shred the goat and stir together with the remaining sauce.

Preheat the oven to 350°F.

To build the enchiladas, use a 9 x 13 glass baking dish. Take a tortilla and spoon a little of the ancho chili sauce over the surface to soften the tortilla. Place some of the goat meat down the middle of the tortilla add a little of the crumbled goat cheese to the meat, making sure it is just enough to still roll the tortilla. Roll the tortilla with the filling and place seam-side down in the 9 x 13 glass baking dish. Repeat the process with the remaining tortillas until the pan is full. Spoon the remaining reserved ancho chili sauce over the enchiladas. Place in the oven and bake for 15 to 20 minutes, or until hot. Remove from the oven and garnish with the remaining goat cheese and cilantro.

WINE SUGGESTION:

Wagner Vineyards Estate Winery, Semi-dry Riesling, Finger Lakes, New York

Riesling is often regarded as the "golden child" of Finger Lakes grape-growers. Comprised of four different Riesling clones, this superbly balanced Riesling is bursting with lively acidity, citrus flavors, and hints of stonefruit. From lifelong local residents to first-time visitors to cross-country loyalists, Wagner Vineyards' Semi-dry Riesling pleases a variety of palates and appeals to wine lovers across the country.

Red Wine-Braised Goat Shanks

Serves 4

2 large goat shanks

Salt and fresh cracked black
pepper, as needed

2–3 tablespoons all-purpose
flour

2–3 tablespoons high-heat
cooking oil (grapeseed), as
needed

8 shallots, peeled and roughly
chopped

2 carrots, roughly chopped

1 celery stalk, roughly chopped

1 leek (white and light green
parts only), roughly chopped

4 garlic cloves, peeled and
smashed

4 cups red wine (Cabernet
Sauvignon)

1 (14½-ounce) can crushed
tomatoes

4 bay leaves

4 sprigs fresh thyme

8 cups chicken stock

Preheat the oven to 350°F.

Generously season the goat shanks with the salt and pepper. Then dust them thoroughly in the flour. Preheat a Dutch oven or similar-sized pot to medium heat. Add the oil to the pot and sear the goat shanks on all sides. Remove the shanks from the pot and place them on a plate. If needed, add additional oil to the pot, then add the shallots, carrots, celery, leek, and garlic and begin to sweat. Lightly caramelize the vegetables, which will take 3 to 5 minutes. Add the red wine, increase the heat to medium-high, and reduce the 4 cups of red wine to 1. Once reduced, add the crushed tomatoes, bay leaves, fresh thyme, and chicken stock and stir well. Add the goat shanks back to the pot and bring to a low simmer. Place the lid on the pot or make a tight foil lid and place in the oven. Braise for 2½ to 3½ hours, rotating the shanks every 45 minutes. Stir the braising liquid when rotating the shanks. When fork-tender, remove the shanks and place on a plate. Also remove all of the other vegetables and herbs from the pot and discard them, then reduce the liquid in the pot by half by boiling it. Make sure to stir the pot regularly so it doesn't caramelize on the bottom and burn. Place the shanks back into the sauce and coat them well. Place the shanks on a platter, spoon the sauce over top, and enjoy with sides such as mashed potatoes or creamy Parmesan polenta.

WINE SUGGESTION:

Wagner Vineyards Estate Winery, Cabernet Sauvignon, Finger Lakes, New York

Wagner Vineyards' full-bodied and food-friendly Cabernet Sauvignon is loaded with aromas of cedar, black currants, and plums. Aging in a combination of new and older small oak barrels contributes to this wine's supple mouthfeel.

Yellow Goat Coconut Curry

Serves 4

2 pounds goat meat, cut into 2-inch
pieces

Kosher salt and fresh cracked black
pepper

¼ cup + 2 tablespoons yellow curry
powder, divided

2–3 tablespoons coconut oil

2 yellow onions, peeled and finely
chopped

¼ cup peeled and finely minced
garlic

¼ cup peeled and finely minced
ginger

1 cup white wine

2 (14½-ounce) can cream of coconut

4 bay leaves

1 cup red bell pepper, seeded and
chopped into 1-inch pieces

1 cup carrots cut in half-moon slices

½ cup chopped scallions

1 lime, zested and juiced

Rice, as needed, cooked according to
package directions, for serving

1 cup fresh cilantro, roughly chopped

The night before cooking, generously season the goat with salt and pepper in a large bowl. Then dust the goat with the ¼ cup of yellow curry powder. Cover with plastic wrap and let sit in fridge overnight to cure.

Preheat the oven to 350°F.

The next day, heat a large pan over medium-high heat. Add the coconut oil and sear the goat. You may need to do this in batches, transferring the caramelized goat in a bowl once finished. Turn the pan down to medium, and add the onions, garlic, and ginger. Sweat the vegetables and don't let them caramelize too much. Once translucent and soft, add the 2 tablespoons of yellow curry powder to the pan and cook for 1 to 2 minutes, deglazing with the wine and reducing by half. Add the cream of coconut, bay leaves, and goat to the pan and stir. Cover the pan with a tight lid, place the pan in the oven, and cook for 2 to 3 hours, or until the goat is almost fork-tender.

Add the red bell pepper, carrots, and scallions and cook for another 30 minutes until the carrots are tender and the goat can be shredded with a fork. Right before serving, add the zest of 1 lime and its juice to the pan and stir together.

Serve over rice and garnish with the chopped cilantro.

WINE SUGGESTION:

Wagner Vineyards Estate Winery, Dry Riesling, Finger Lakes, New York

Wagner's Dry Riesling is mineral-driven on the nose and all fruit on the palate. Lime peel, apple, and pears combined with well-balanced acidity makes for a bright wine with a lasting finish. Comprised of numerous Riesling blocks, this fresh and full-bodied wine is the perfect enhancement to a wide array of meals.

Butchering
Hog & Pig

Similar to the Lamb, Sheep & Goat chapter, when preparing for the humane, timely, and tidy dispatch of a hog or pig, foremost we must plan for the considerations of "set and setting." For example: Where on the farm or homestead will the slaughter site be located? What time of day? How many people will be helping? What tasks will be assigned to which people, and with what available tools?

The professional mobile butcher will possess full knowledge of the vast minutiae of all that can go wrong and will plan for and arrange each job in a manner that leaves the least room for error and provides the greatest opportunity for a successful result. As amateur home butchers, we can pick apart a few of the most important concepts and considerations of the professional butcher, and thereby increase the likelihood of attaining a successful and positive home-kill experience.

Preparation and animal handling:

- Corral the animal(s) and withhold feed for twenty-four hours prior to the planned slaughter date.
- Make sure the animal has continual access to water.
- When knocking an animal, having close proximity to the animal is ideal. Experienced slaughtermen will always prefer knocking a calm animal at close range. Great lengths should be taken to ensure the animal is corralled comfortably and is very calm prior to knocking.

Knocking tools:

- There are many makes and models of firearms and captive bolt guns that can successfully knock a hog when discharged at the appropriate distance. Always have a backup plan and ideally a loaded backup firearm should the first shot not drop the animal.
- A captive bolt gun is a good choice for knocking if a firearm is not practical or legal at the slaughter site.
- A .22 mag is appropriate for most medium and small pigs when discharged at a very close range. Older hogs, larger hogs, sows, and boars will have thicker/harder skulls, and therefore a more powerful firearm will be desirable to ensure the animal drops with one shot.

Additional tools:

- Knives: lamb skinner knife used for skinning, jointing, and gutting. Also a 5- to 6-inch boning knife and beef skinner knife used for trimming.
- Halter (optional) for walking the animal to the knocking site and/or for controlling the animal's head position during knocking.
- Carabiner (optional) and California hook connected to a waistband to fix the foreleg into position during foreleg skinning.
- Bone saw to saw pelvis.
- Hoist, winch, or tractor for lifting the carcass.
- Two plywood 4x4s (or any other implement) for cradling the carcass into position on the ground if needed for a larger hog such as a sow or boar.

- Gambrel and strap, chain, or rope for hoisting from hind legs.
- Thin wire or rope (optional) for postmortem hog-tying legs and/or tractoring carcass.
- Water source. Ideally a hose but also a bucket of water.
- Barrel to put gut contents in, if needed, to remove from the slaughter site.
- A vinegar solution spray of 2.5 percent vinegar to water (optional) for cleaning purposes.

Slaughter site:

- The ideal slaughter site has mostly to do with convenience, ease of handling, and ensuring calmness of the animal. The slaughtermen may also want to consider the drainage and accessibility of the site. Will the water and blood be able to drain easily from the site? Can a water hose reach the site? If not, can buckets filled with water be used for washing and cleanliness? Can a tractor or truck access the site easily without getting stuck? If power is needed, can an extension cord reach the site?

Knocking tips:

- If the farmer has knowledge of which hog is the leader hog among a group of multiple hogs, kill this lead hog last. The lead hog will be most relaxed when the rest of the hogs have been dispatched. Hogs that are further down in the hierarchy will be very distraught (and thereby harder to shoot) if their comrades have been killed and they are deprived of their social support system.

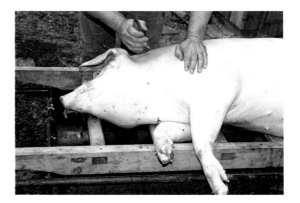

- Study diagrams and attempt to memorize the position of the hog's brain. Visualize the brain location before approaching the animal. Remember the brain extends from the spinal cord, so it is useful to look at the animal's neck and draw an imaginary line upward from the line of the spinal cord toward the skull.
- Hog skull geometry can vary greatly from breed to breed. Do not attempt to take a shot until you have taken a close look at the animal and have a clear idea of where the brain is positioned.
- Knocking can occur from any number of positions in front, behind, or to the side of the skull, as long as the bullet is directed toward the brain. Most commonly pigs are knocked from the forehead.

Check for signs of insensibility:

- The head and neck should be loose and floppy.
- Eyes should be open with a blank stare. No eye movement or blinking.
- Tongue should hang out limply.
- No vocalization of the animal, and no response to poking the animal's nose.
- The tail should be relaxed and hang limply.

Bleeding the pig:

- Postmortem rigidity will set in quicker for hogs as compared to other animals. Therefore, skinning and gutting should commence without long periods of delay once the animal has bled out.
- Position the body into the direction where you would like the blood to flow.
- Extend the head/neck of the animal to tighten the neck skin and put yourself into a position where you will not be kicked as the animal's nervous system may cause it to thrash about.
- A good "stick" will appear to gush blood and not merely ooze.

Hoist and cradle:

- If the hog is heavy, hog-tie it and mechanically hoist it to the area where it will be dressed out.
- Especially in the case of a large sow or boar, the dead animal will need to be supported either using a beef cradle, or on the ground using implements such as tires or plywood 4x4s positioned at either side. The goal is for the hog to be supported so the animal is lying on its back with all four legs up in the air.
- Medium and small pigs may not need a cradle. While the slaughterman skins the hind legs, they can straddle the shoulders of the animal and thereby steady the pig using the slaughterman's feet and legs to support.

Skin forelegs and remove foreleg trotter section:

- Hogskin is best opened using a lamb skinner knife. The flanks are easily skinned using a beef skinner knife.
- The goal of hog skinning is to remove only the skin and leave all of the fat and muscle on the carcass.
- Open the forelegs skin beginning at the dewclaw. (A California hook may be used to create tension at the dewclaw while skinning. In the absence of a California hook setup, the trotter can be pinched between the knees to create tension while skinning.)
- Cut a line from the dewclaw along the inside of the forelegs, connecting these lines at the sternum.
- Skin the entire forelegs and remove the foreleg trotter.
- Cut a line from the snout, along the midline of the neck, sternum, and belly, through the anus and into the tail.
- At the hind legs, insert a lamb skinner knife into the dewclaw and cut along the inside of the hams, connecting these lines together at the rump.
- Skin the front and back of the hind legs as much as is possible while cradled.
- Saw open the sternum at this time.
- Using a beef skinner knife, skin the head, neck, shoulders, flanks, and rump of the pig, all the way down to where the back of the animal where the ground/cradle is located.
- After skinning the belly and flanks, if the pig is male, remove the pizzle.

- Insert the gambrel at the hind shank between the shank and Achilles tendon, and hoist.

Gambrel, hoist, and remove hind trotter section:

- Hoist the pig so that it is inverted but you can still reach the hind trotters.
- Remove the hind trotters at the joint or by sawing near the joint. Take great care to avoid damaging the Achilles tendon.
- Continue hoisting until the snout is an inch from the ground.

Finish skinning:

- Cut between the tail and the last lumbar vertebra. Continue skinning below the tail into the low back area of the hog.
- Once you have separated the tail and skinned a few inches below the tail, grab the tail and forcefully pull the entire hogskin down toward the head of the animal. The skin should peel away from the fat all the way down to the shoulder area.
- Using a lamb skinner or beef skinner knife, finish skinning the shoulder, neck, and head area of the pig.
- Take care at the snout because pig teeth can dull your blade easily.

Prepare for gutting and removal:

- Trim the hams if necessary (removing hair, dirt, etc.) and saw open the pelvis bone.
- With a knife, open the first few inches of the stomach at the midline nearest to the pelvis. This will allow the belly area to slightly pull away from the intestine and stomach area.

- Cut *around* the bung to loosen the connections at the anal canal. Do not cut into the anal canal.
- Once the anal canal is loosened, pull down toward the animal's underbelly with one hand. If needed, wrap a towel around the bung opening to avoid oozing feces on the carcass.
- Perform a midline belly opening cut with your fist in between the stomach and the internal belly wall, and the knife pointed outward. Cut down, opening the belly the entire length and connecting your cut line to the open sternum.

Pork: Recipes & Wine Pairings

The following recipes are graciously provided by the National Pork Board.

The National Pork Board is an organization that works toward uniting pork producers to build a bright future for the US pork industry. Congress created the Pork Checkoff as part of the Pork Promotion, Research and Consumer Information Act of 1985. In 1987, the Board introduced its "Pork. The Other White Meat" slogan as a means of promoting pork as a lean meat to health-conscious consumers. Today, the National Pork Board continues to execute specific programs in the areas of pork promotion, research and education.

Accompanying each recipe are suggested wine pairings provided by Chateau Ste. Michelle.

Founded in 1934, Chateau Ste. Michelle pioneered vinifera grape growing in Washington State and has been producing classic European varietal wines under the Ste. Michelle label since 1967. The winery combines an ongoing dedication to research with a commitment to classic winemaking traditions. The winery owns 3,900 acres of vineyards in the Columbia Valley of Eastern Washington, including Canoe Ridge Estate and Cold Creek, which are LIVE and Salmon Safe certified. Chateau Ste. Michelle also enjoys winemaking partnerships with some of the world's most distinguished vintners.

Boneless Pork Loin Roast with Herbed Pepper Rub

Serves 12

Serve this as part of a casual New Year's Eve celebration buffet.

1 (3-pound) boneless pork loin roast
2 tablespoons cracked black pepper
2 tablespoons grated Parmesan cheese
2 teaspoons dried basil
2 teaspoons dried rosemary
2 teaspoons dried thyme
¼ teaspoon garlic powder
¼ teaspoon salt

Pat the pork dry with paper towel.

Preheat the oven to 350°F.

In small bowl, combine the pepper, cheese, basil, rosemary, thyme, garlic powder, and salt. Apply liberally to all surfaces of the pork roast. Place the roast in a shallow pan and roast in the oven for 1 hour (20 minutes per pound), until the internal temperature on a meat thermometer reads 145°F. Remove the roast from the oven and let rest about 10 minutes before slicing to serve.

WINE SUGGESTION:

Chateau Ste. Michelle Canoe Ridge Estate Merlot

This Canoe Ridge Estate Merlot consistently exhibits elegance, concentration, and fine tannins. The wine also exhibits dark cherry fruit, with an opulent mouthfeel and structure. Winemaker Bob Bertheau enjoys matching the Canoe Ridge Merlot with a variety of Italian dishes.

Country-Style Ribs
with Peach Rosemary Glaze

Serves 6

These country-style ribs are great for backyard cookouts. Serve them alongside tangy baked beans or cool coleslaw.

2 pounds boneless country-style
   pork ribs, individually cut
2 tablespoons canola oil
2 teaspoons dried rosemary
1 tablespoon fresh rosemary
1½ teaspoons coarse salt
1 teaspoon coarsely ground
   black pepper
½ cup peach preserves, warmed
   until softened

Brush the ribs with the oil.

In small bowl, combine the rosemary, salt, and pepper. Season the ribs all over with the rosemary mixture. Let stand for 30 minutes.

Preheat an outdoor grill for direct, medium-high heat (page 17).

Place the ribs on the prepared grill over indirect heat (not directly over the heat source) and close the lid. Grill for 35 to 45 minutes, or until the ribs are tender. During the last 15 minutes of grilling, baste the ribs on all sides occasionally with the warmed peach preserves. Remove from grill and let rest 3 minutes before serving.

WINE SUGGESTION:

Chateau Ste. Michelle Columbia Valley Syrah

The Columbia Valley Syrah is a soft, jammy Syrah made in an approachable and fruit-forward style. This is an enjoyable, easy-to-drink red.

Tangy Grilled Back Ribs

Serves 4

Simply grilled slow and low with a flavorful kick of sauce the last 15 minutes of grilling. Serve these tangy ribs with backyard favorites of potato salad, deviled eggs, cucumber salad, and icy watermelon.

4 pounds pork back ribs
Salt and cracked black pepper,
  as needed
1 cup reduced-fat French
  dressing
2 tablespoons onion soup mix
2 tablespoons honey
1 tablespoon reduced-sodium
  soy sauce

Season the ribs with salt and pepper.

Preheat an outdoor grill for direct, medium-high heat (page 17).

Place the ribs on the prepared grill over indirect heat (not directly over the heat source) and close the lid. Grill for 1½ to 2 hours, or until the ribs are tender.

In a small bowl, combine the dressing, soup mix, honey, and soy sauce in a small bowl. Let stand 15 minutes or until needed.

Brush the ribs with sauce during the last 15 to 30 minutes of cooking. Serve the ribs with a side of the remaining sauce.

WINE SUGGESTION:

Chateau Ste. Michelle Indian Wells Red Blend

The Indian Wells Red Blend is an easy-to-enjoy red from warmer-climate vineyards. The wine reflects the rich, round powerful style of Washington fruit, highlighting nine varietals. It is a true example of the art of blending. The wine offers jammy boysenberry flavors from the Syrah with a luscious concentration from the Merlot. This would be a great match with barbecued ribs.

Honey and Sage-Roasted Rack of Pork

Serves 16

Nothing is more memorable than the unexpected. This rack of pork is perfect for those large holiday gatherings. Serve with a Waldorf salad, Brussels sprouts, and garlic rosemary mashed potatoes, and finish with cherry pie.

2 racks pork rib rack, 8 ribs each, center cut, chine bone off, frenched

Salt and cracked black pepper, as needed

½ cup honey

2 tablespoons fresh sage, snipped

Season the pork racks with salt and pepper.

Preheat the oven to 350°F.

Place each rack in roasting pans with the bones facing up and sides not touching. Roast in the oven for 1 to 1½ hours (20 minutes per pound) until the internal temperature on a meat thermometer reads 145°F. Remove the roast from oven and let rest about 10 minutes.

In a small bowl, stir together the honey and sage. Brush the honey-sage mixture onto the roast after removing from the oven and serve.

WINE SUGGESTION:

Chateau Ste. Michelle Cold Creek Cab

Cabernet from this iconic forty-five-year-old vineyard consistently delivers power, structure and rich concentrated black fruit. The wine offers black cherry flavors and chocolate notes with typical Cold Creek density and user-friendly power. This is 100 percent Cabernet because Cold Creek Cab shines on its own.

Barbecue Pork Skillet

Serves 4

This is a quick way to serve up tangy barbecue flavor in a hurry from your stovetop. Serve these saucy chops with warm dinner rolls and coleslaw.

4 New York–style pork chops,
   ¾-inch thick
1 teaspoon vegetable oil
¼ cup Italian salad dressing
¼ cup barbecue sauce

Pat the chops dry with paper towel.

Heat the oil in a large skillet over medium-high heat until hot. Add the chops and brown about 1 minute on each side. Add the dressing and barbecue sauce to the pan, stirring to blend. Cover and simmer for 5 to 8 minutes, or until the internal temperature on a meat thermometer reads 145°F. Remove from heat and let rest for about 3 minutes before serving.

WINE SUGGESTION:

Chateau Ste. Michelle Columbia Valley Syrah

Winemaker Bob Bertheau describes the Columbia Valley Syrah as a soft, jammy Syrah made in an approachable and fruit-forward style. This is an enjoyable, easy-to-drink red.

Pork and Zucchini Stew

Serves 6

Have extra zucchini from your garden? Did the neighbor's zucchini vine have a bumper crop? Try this stew with some bread and a side salad.

3 boneless pork chops, cut into ¾-inch cubes

3 tablespoons flour

½ teaspoon garlic salt

½ teaspoon cracked black pepper

1 tablespoon vegetable oil

1 medium onion, peeled and chopped

1 green bell pepper, seeded and chopped

4 cups fresh mushrooms, cleaned and sliced

1 (29-ounce) can stewed tomatoes, undrained

2 medium zucchini, halved lengthwise and sliced ½-inch thick

2 teaspoons dried basil

1 teaspoon dried oregano

⅓ cup grated Parmesan cheese

Pat the pork cubes dry with paper towel.

In a plastic or paper bag, combine the flour, garlic salt, and pepper. Add the pork cubes and shake until well coated with the flour mixture. Set aside.

In a Dutch oven, heat the oil over medium-high heat until hot. Add the onion and bell pepper and cook until the onion is tender but not brown. Add the pork and cook, stirring, for 2 to 3 minutes or until browned. Stir in the mushrooms, tomatoes, zucchini, basil, and oregano. Bring to boiling, then reduce heat. Cover and simmer for 10 to 15 minutes or until the pork is tender, stirring occasionally. Remove from the heat.

To serve, spoon the Pork and Zucchini Stew into individual soup bowls. Sprinkle with Parmesan cheese and serve.

WINE SUGGESTION:

Chateau Ste. Michelle Indian Wells Merlot

The Indian Wells Merlot offers ripe berry fruit aromas and jammy flavors. This is a full-bodied style of warm-climate Merlot with a round, supple finish. Winemaker Bob Bertheau adds Wahluke Slope Syrah to enhance the mouthfeel and rich fruit character. He calls this his "pasta wine."

Pork Tenderloin Diane

Serves 4

Nothing could be easier—or more elegant—than this French preparation for sautéed steak, borrowed here for pork tenderloin. Quickly sautéed fillet medallions are finished with a Worcestershire sauce and mustard pan sauce. If it is a special occasion, pair this dish with truffled mashed potatoes and steamed asparagus. If it's a weeknight, mashed potatoes and green peas will fit the bill. Add a green salad with vinaigrette and warm dinner rolls.

1 pork tenderloin, cut into
    8 crosswise pieces
2 teaspoons lemon pepper
1 tablespoon butter
1 tablespoon fresh lemon juice
1 tablespoon Worcestershire
    sauce
1 teaspoon Dijon-style mustard
1 tablespoon fresh Italian
    parsley, minced

Place each piece of tenderloin between 2 pieces of plastic wrap. Flatten slightly with the heel of your hand. Sprinkle the surfaces of pork with the lemon pepper.

Heat the butter in heavy nonstick skillet. Add the pork and brown evenly, about 3 to 4 minutes on each side. Remove to a serving platter and keep warm.

Add the lemon juice, Worcestershire sauce, and mustard to the skillet. Cook, stirring with the pan juices, until heated through.

To serve, pour the sauce over the pork, and sprinkle with the parsley.

WINE SUGGESTION:

Chateau Ste. Michelle Columbia Valley Cabernet Sauvignon

This celebrated winery crafts their Columbia Valley Cabernet to highlight concentrated Washington red fruit in an accessible style. This is an inviting Cab with plenty of complexity and structure with silky tannins. It's also very versatile with food. Enjoy it with beef tenderloin or pasta.

Stir-Fried Pork in Garlic Sauce

Serves 4

Simple stir-fry for a quick weeknight meal. Have everything prepared before cooking. Serve with a seasonally fresh fruit salad.

1½ pounds pork tenderloin or shoulder, cut into thin shreds
2 tablespoons peanut or vegetable oil
2 tablespoons garlic, peeled and chopped
2 dried chilies
1 bunch scallions, trimmed and cut into 2-inch lengths; separate the white parts from the green parts
3 tablespoons soy sauce
4 cups cooked white rice

Pat the pork dry with paper towel.

Put the oil in a large, nonstick skillet (12 inches is best). Turn the heat to high, and one minute later add the garlic and chilies. Cook, stirring occasionally, until the garlic begins to color, about 1 minute. Add the pork and stir once or twice. Cook until the meat begins to brown, about 1 minute. Add the white parts of the scallions and stir. Cook another minute, stirring occasionally. Stir in the green parts of the scallions and stir. Cook for 30 seconds, then turn off the heat and add the soy sauce. Serve immediately with white rice.

WINE SUGGESTION:

Chateau Ste. Michelle & Dr. Loosen Eroica Riesling

Eroica Riesling offers sweet lime and mandarin orange aromas with subtle mineral notes. The mouthwatering acidity is beautifully balanced by flavorful Washington Riesling fruit. Eroica is a blended statement of the finest Riesling vineyards in the state. To achieve our Eroica style, the winery strives for bright fruit with crisp acidity and enhanced minerality.

"Sweet Fire" Porterhouse Pork Chops

Serves 4

Enjoy these pork chops with mashed sweet potatoes and sautéed green beans.

4 porterhouse pork chops, about
¾-inch thick
2 tablespoons olive oil
1½ teaspoons ground chipotle
chili
1½ teaspoons coarse salt
1 large orange, zested
2 teaspoons minced garlic
⅓ cup honey

Pat dry the pork with paper towel.

In a small bowl, stir the oil, ground chipotle, salt, orange zest, and garlic together into a paste. Using a rubber spatula, spread the chipotle mixture over both sides of the pork. Let stand for 15 to 30 minutes.

Preheat an outdoor grill for direct, medium-high heat (page 17).

Place the chops on the prepared grill over direct heat (yes, directly over the heat source) and close the lid. Grill about 4 to 5 minutes per side, turning once, until the internal temperature of the pork on a meat thermometer measures between 145°F (medium rare) and 160°F (medium). During the last 2 minutes, brush the chops on both sides with the honey. Remove the chops from the grill and let rest for 3 minutes before serving.

WINE SUGGESTION:

Domaine Ste. Michelle Brut

Delicate aromas of green apple; bright citrus notes with a persistent bubble and balanced acidity. Domaine Ste. Michelle Brut is the perfect accompaniment for a wide array of foods.

Smoky Pork, Bacon, and White Bean Chili

Serves 6

To make this chili even more smolderingly smoky, add a finely chopped chipotle chili (from a can of chipotles in adobo sauce) along with the onion, or add some cayenne powder along with the chili powder. You can also cook this recipe in a slow cooker—start it in a large skillet, then just before adding the tomatoes, transfer everything to a slow cooker and proceed from there in the slow cooker. On the side, serve warm tortillas, tortilla chips, corn bread, or a green salad with radishes, avocado, and cilantro.

1½ pounds pork loin roast, cut into ¾-inch dice

8 ounces thick-cut bacon, 5 or 6 slices, cut crosswise into ¼-inch strips

1 large onion, peeled and cut into ½-inch dice

2 tablespoons chili powder

1 tablespoon smoked paprika

1 (29-ounce) can diced fire-roasted tomatoes, juice reserved

1½ cups water

1 (30-ounce) can cannellini beans, white kidney, or other white beans, drained

Salt, to taste

½ cup sour cream, optional

2 scallions, thinly sliced, optional

Pat the pork dry with paper towel.

In a large saucepan or small stockpot over medium heat, cook the bacon, stirring occasionally, until crisp, 8 to 10 minutes. Use a slotted spoon to transfer the bacon to a paper towel–lined plate and set aside.

Add the onion to the bacon fat and cook, stirring occasionally, for 2 minutes. Increase the heat to medium-high and add the pork. Cook, stirring occasionally, until the onion is crisp-tender, 6 to 8 minutes. Stir in the chili powder and paprika. Stir in the tomatoes (with their juice) and water. Bring to a boil, reduce to a simmer, and cook, stirring occasionally, until the pork is tender, 35 to 45 minutes.

Stir in the beans and about ⅔ of the bacon and cook, stirring occasionally, until heated through, about 10 minutes. Add salt to taste. Serve the chili garnished with the remaining bacon and the sour cream and scallions, if using.

WINE SUGGESTION:

Chateau Ste. Michelle Canoe Ridge Estate Chardonnay

The Canoe Ridge Estate Chardonnay is refined and elegant and offers apple and citrus aromas with a clean, refreshing finish. The Pacific Northwest winery ages the wine in lighter French oak barrels to maintain the fresh, elegant style of this Chardonnay.

Pepper & Pineapple Pork Stew

Serves 4

A tasty and colorful pork stew that cooks while you are out. Serve with hot cooked brown rice and breadsticks.

4 pork chops, boneless, cut into 1-inch cubes
1 teaspoon vegetable oil
4 carrots, sliced
½ cup chicken broth
3 tablespoons teriyaki sauce
1 tablespoon cornstarch
1 (8-ounce) can pineapple chunks, drained, reserving juice
1 green bell pepper, seeded and cut into 1-inch pieces

Pat the pork dry with paper towel.

Plug in a slow cooker and set to Low cooking.

Heat the oil in a large skillet over medium-high heat until hot. Add the pork cubes and cook until brown on all sides. Transfer the pork to the slow cooker and add the carrots, broth, and teriyaki sauce. Cover and cook for 7 to 8 hours.

Before serving, in a small bowl, combine the cornstarch with the reserved pineapple juice. Add to the slow cooker. Stir in the pineapple and green pepper. Cover and set the slow cooker to High. Cook for 15 minutes, or until the sauce is thickened and bubbly. Turn off the heat and serve.

WINE SUGGESTION:

Chateau Ste. Michelle Columbia Valley Gewürztraminer

A fan favorite, the winery's Gewürztraminer is a flavorful wine with bright, expressive fruit and clove spice. This is a lush style of Gewürztraminer with intense floral character, yet it still maintains the grape's natural crisp acidity. Try this wine with Thai food or any cuisine with a little bite to it.

Herbed Butterfly Pork Chops

Serves 4

Use your herb garden for this basic chop. Simply change the flavor by changing the herbs. The cooking time is the same for grilling and for broiling. Serve with coleslaw, steamed green beans, and garlic mashed potatoes.

4 butterflied pork chops, 4 ounces each

2 tablespoons fresh lemon juice

2 tablespoons chopped fresh Italian parsley

½ teaspoon crumbled fresh rosemary

½ teaspoon crumbled fresh thyme

¼ teaspoon cracked black pepper

Brush the chops with lemon juice.

In a small bowl, combine the parsley, rosemary, thyme, and pepper. Rub the herb mixture on both sides of the chops.

Preheat an outdoor grill for direct, medium-high heat (page x).

Place the chops on the grill over direct heat (yes, directly over the heat source) and close the lid. Grill about 8 to 9 minutes per side, turning occasionally, until the internal temperature of the pork on a meat thermometer measures between 145°F (medium rare) and 160°F (medium). Remove the chops from the heat and let rest for about 3 minutes before serving. Garnish with fresh herbs, if desired.

WINE SUGGESTION:

Chateau Ste. Michelle Columbia Valley Merlot

The Washington State winery crafts this wine to be their complex yet approachable Merlot. The wine offers aromas of black cherry, leather, and spice with layers of rich dark red fruit flavors and a long, smooth, sweet finish. A touch of Syrah adds a jammy fruit character. Winemaker Bob Bertheau believes this wine to be a great "everyday red."

Italian Pork Melts

Serves 4

This dish works well with leftover pork. Make sure if younger cooks are helping to have an adult use the broiler.

1 pound boneless pork roast, sliced into stir-fry strips
2 teaspoons olive oil
½ cup nonfat mayonnaise
4 submarine rolls, 6-inch, split
⅔ cup pesto
2 whole roasted red peppers, drained and halved
4 ounces mozzarella cheese

Pat the pork dry with paper towel.

Turn the oven to broil.

Heat the oil in a large nonstick skillet over medium-high heat. Add the pork strips to the pan and brown while stir-frying. Remove from heat.

While the pork cooks, spread the mayonnaise on the bottom half of the rolls. Spread the pesto on the top halves of the rolls. Place the rolls under the broiler briefly to lightly brown. Remove from oven.

Divide the pork strips onto the four roll halves and top with the peppers and cheese. Return to under the broiler and broil until the cheese is bubbly. Remove from the oven and add the other roll halves to make sandwiches. Serve hot.

WINE SUGGESTION:

Chateau Ste. Michelle Columbia Valley Sauvignon Blanc

Stainless-steel fermentation makes this a crisp sauvignon blanc. The wine offers bright fruit character of melons and herbs. This wine is also a favorite with oysters.

Orange-Glazed Leg of Pork

Serves 8

This flavorful glaze is also great for glazing a roast pork tenderloin, pork loin roast, or for pork chops on the grill. Serve sliced pork roast with mashed potatoes, buttered green beans, hot French bread, and peach cobbler.

4 pounds boneless leg of pork
12 ounces orange marmalade
1 tablespoon soy sauce
¼ teaspoon ground ginger
¼ teaspoon ground cloves

Heat the oven to 350°F.

Pat the pork dry with paper towel and place in a shallow roasting pan.

In small bowl, stir together the marmalade, soy sauce, ginger, and cloves.

Place the pork in the oven for 1 hour (about 15 minutes per pound), until internal temperature on a thermometer reads 145°F. Brush with marmalade mixture several times during the last 30 minutes of cooking. Remove the roast from the oven and let rest 10 minutes before serving.

WINE SUGGESTION:

Chateau Ste. Michelle Dry Riesling

The Chateau Ste. Michelle Dry Riesling is a dry, refreshing style of Riesling with beautiful fruit flavors, crisp acidity, and an elegant finish. It offers inviting sweet citrus aromas and flavors. This is an incredibly versatile food wine.

Pork Tenderloin Sliders with Three Sauces

Serves 12

You can replace the romaine lettuce with arugula, baby greens, baby spinach, or cabbage instead. Make all three sauces so everyone has a choice, or choose your favorite bottled sauce, such as barbecue or honey-mustard sauce. Serve the sliders with baked sweet potato fries.

1 (1-pound) pork tenderloin, trimmed
1 teaspoon salt-free seasoning
2 teaspoons olive oil
12 mini rolls, 1½-x-2 inches, split and toasted
6 romaine lettuce leaves, torn
2 plum tomatoes, each cut into 6 slices
Three Sauces (recipes follow)

Pat the pork dry with paper towel, and then cut the tenderloin into ½-inch-thick slices. Sprinkle the pork on all sides with the seasoning.

Heat the oil in a large heavy skillet over medium-high heat. Add the pork and cook, turning once, until the pork is browned, about 1½ minutes on each side.

Place the tenderloin in the rolls, and top with lettuce, tomatoes, and the sauces of your choice.

WINE SUGGESTION:

Chateau Ste. Michelle Columbia Valley Rosé

The Chateau Ste. Michelle Columbia Valley Rosé is a dry elegant rosé with a beautiful light pale pink color. The fresh and lively wine offers bright aromas of watermelon and raspberry with flavors of wild strawberry, citrus zest, and hints of melon. It is soft and flavorful on the palate with a long, crisp finish.

YOGURT-LIME SAUCE
Makes ½ cup

½ cup low-fat plain Greek
  yogurt
½ teaspoon grated lime zest
2 teaspoons fresh lime juice
1 tablespoon fresh cilantro,
  chopped

In a small bowl, add the yogurt, lime zest, lime juice, and cilantro.
Stir until well mixed.

SPICY AVOCADO SAUCE

Makes a ½ cup + 1 tablespoon

1 small ripe avocado, halved,
  pitted, and peeled
1 tablespoon jalapeño pepper,
  minced, including seeds
1 tablespoon fresh lime juice
2 teaspoons fresh cilantro,
  minced

Place the avocado in a small bowl and mash with a fork or potato
masher until smooth. Add the jalapeño, lime juice, and cilantro.
Stir until well mixed.

GOAT CHEESE-BASIL SAUCE

Makes a ½ cup

½ cup (4 ounces) soft goat
  cheese, room temperature
1 tablespoon fresh basil,
  chopped
1 garlic clove, peeled and
  minced
1 teaspoon fresh lemon juice
1 pinch black pepper

In a small bowl, add the goat cheese, basil, garlic, lemon juice, and
pepper. Stir until well mixed.

Butchering Cattle

Like the Hogs & Pigs chapter, when preparing for the humane, timely, and tidy dispatch of a beef animal, foremost we must plan for the considerations of "set and setting." For example, where on the farm or homestead will the slaughter site be located? What time of day? How many people will be helping? What tasks will be assigned to which people, and with what available tools?

The professional mobile butcher will possess full knowledge of the vast minutiae of all that can go wrong and will plan for and arrange each job in a manner that leaves the least room for error and provides the greatest opportunity for a successful result. As amateur home butchers, we can pick apart a few of the most important concepts and considerations of the professional butcher, thereby increasing the likelihood of attaining a successful and positive home-kill experience.

Preparation and animal handling:

- Corral the animal(s) and withhold feed for twenty-four hours prior to the planned slaughter date.
- Make sure the animal has continual access to water.
- When knocking an animal, having close proximity to the animal is ideal. Experienced slaughtermen will always prefer knocking a calm animal at close range. Great lengths should be taken to ensure the animal is corralled comfortably and is very calm prior to knocking.

Knocking tools:

- There are many makes and models of firearms and captive bolt guns that can successfully knock a beef when discharged at the appropriate distance. Always have a backup plan and ideally a loaded backup firearm should the first shot not drop the animal.
- The thickness of the animal's forehead will determine which caliber firearm to use. Bulls, especially older bulls, and larger beeves will have the thickest foreheads. Every precaution must be taken to ensure the firearm is sufficiently powerful and the bullet does not merely glance off the forehead of the animal.

Additional tools:

- Splitting Tools: A battery-powered Sawzall is often used by mobile slaughtermen in the field. A Jarvis Wellsaw can serve as an effective splitting tool, one that requires an extension cord. A two-handed cleaver can also be used along one side of the featherbones after marking the line with a knife. A chain saw works fine too when using food-grade oil instead of bar oil.

- Knives: A beef skinner is used for skinning, a lamb skinner is used for jointing, and a boning knife is used for trimming.
- Butcher's twine for tying weasand, bung, and neck skin.
- Plastic bag for bung.
- Hoist, winch, or tractor for lifting the carcass.
- Two plywood 4x4s (or any other implement) for cradling the carcass into position on the ground (the jointed hooves can also be used for this).
- Gambrel and strap, chain, or rope for hoisting.
- Water source. Ideally a hose but also a bucket of water.
- Barrel to put stomach contents in, if needed, to remove from the slaughter site.
- A vinegar solution spray of 2.5 percent vinegar to water (optional) for cleaning purposes.

Slaughter site:

- The ideal slaughter site has mostly to do with convenience, ease of handling, and ensuring calmness of the animal. The slaughtermen may also want to consider the drainage and accessibility of the site. Will the water and blood be able to drain easily from the site? Can a water hose reach the site? If not, can buckets filled with water be used for washing and cleanliness? Can a tractor or truck access the site easily without getting stuck? If power is needed, can an extension cord reach the site?

Knocking tips:

- There are many techniques butchers will employ in the moments leading up to pulling the trigger. The goal is to get the animal to look straight at the slaughterman and hold its head still. A headgate can be used if available to fix the animal's head in the desired position. If using a captive bolt, then the slaughterman must be in a position adjacent to and slightly above the animal, and the captive bolt gun must come to rest touching the target area on the animal's forehead.
- When using a firearm at short or long distance, the slaughterman must learn how to move in such a way so their actions keep the animal relaxed and calm. Prey animals such as cattle are masters of body language. Even when they appear aloof or unaware, they are paying close attention to the movement and subtle cues of the animals and humans around them.
- Once the slaughterman is in position with the firearm pointed at the chosen animal, he/she might try making a series of "clicks" or obscure noises to inspire the curiosity of the chosen animal. By making strange, nonthreatening, curiosity-provoking noises, the slaughterman can cause the animal to look directly at him and hold its head completely still. A curious and calm animal will look at the slaughterman and hesitate, trying to figure out what is happening. This is the ideal opportunity for a head shot. A clean head shot is the result of the slaughterman and farmer together having

cultivated low stress conditions. A good slaughterman will wait as long as it takes for the animal to hold its head still prior to firing.

- In an open field situation, one available technique is for the slaughterman to lay on the ground and take aim from a supine position. Often times just seeing a human laying on the ground will provoke the curiosity of the animal, causing it, in many cases, to not only face the slaughterman, but also to walk toward the slaughterman for an easier shot.

Check for signs of insensibility:
- Head and neck should be loose and floppy.
- Eyes should be open with a blank stare. No eye movement. No blinking.
- Tongue should hang out limply.
- No vocalization of the animal. No response to poking the animal's nose.
- The tail should relax and hang limply.

Bleeding the beef:
- Extend the head/neck of the animal to tighten the neck skin and put yourself into a position where you will not be kicked as the animal's nervous system may cause it to thrash about.
- Ideally within 60 seconds of brain death, the carotid arteries and jugular veins of the animal should be severed to ensure a proper bleed. This is also known as *exsanguination*.
- The "Thoracic Method" of bleeding involves opening the underside of the neck hide, locating the trachea and esophagus, sliding your boning knife along these tubes without severing them, and plunging the knife into the cavity of the animal between the neck and brisket. The ideal outcome will include a large gush of blood as a result of severing the carotid arteries and jugular veins. The esophagus and trachea should not be cut at this stage.

Hoist, remove head, clear and tie weasand:
- Using a chain or heavy-duty strap wrapped around both the hind legs and forelegs between the hooves and knees, hoist the animal into an upside-down position with the back parallel to the ground.
- From this position the head will be hanging down. Now is a good time to hose and scrape the hide in the specific areas you plan on subsequently opening with your knife. If the incision areas are clean prior to cutting, minimal bacteria from the exterior of the hide will drip or smear onto the carcass.
- Starting at the incision made for bleeding, open the hide from the sternum to the middle of jaw, and skin out the head.
- Remove the head at the atlas joint.
- With a clean knife, expose the esophagus (a red tube known as the "weasand") and trachea (white tube used for breathing), and clear these tubes away from the surrounding tissues.
- Separate the trachea from the esophagus with your knife, grasp the esophagus firmly with both hands, and while holding it taut, plunge the leading fist into the cavity of the

neck. The goal is to loosen the esophagus from the surrounding tissues that secure it within the interior of the neck and sternum area. By doing this, the esophagus will slide out effortlessly later on during gutting and will not rip.

Cradle:

- Lower onto a cradle or onto the ground so that the back of the animal is touching the ground and that is all. If not using a beef cradle, wedge plywood 4x4s or some other prop between the ground and the sides so that the animal is balanced and does not slouch over to one side.

Remove hooves:

- Remove forehooves and hind hooves with a knife at the joint, or with a saw at the joint. Pay special attention to cleanliness and trim off any dirt or hair at these sites.
- Great care should be taken to not cause any damage to the Achilles tendon as you trim in preparation for the gambrel.

Skin the rump and sides:

- A beef skinner knife is ideal for this. Leave as much of the cutaneous trunci, or "rose meat" on the carcass as possible.
- Pull at the hide with your non-cutting hand to create optimal tension, thereby making skinning easier.
- Skin as far as you can along both sides, along the rump, and along the upper shoulders and neck. With the animal laying on its back you will not yet be able to skin the back area. This will come later.

- Note: If the beef is a steer, the pizzle should be removed immediately after skinning the sides and rump. If the beef is a cow, the udder should be removed immediately after skinning the sides and rump.

Gambrel hind shanks and partial hoist:

- Take care to trim dirt and hair around the Achilles without damaging the integrity of the Achilles tendon. Gambrel hind legs and hoist the back end off the ground, leaving the front end on the ground.

Open brisket and remove heart:

- While partially hoisted, split the sternum bone open with a bone saw. Take care not to puncture the gut seeing as it will be very near.
- Cut the sac around the heart to locate the heart. Poke a hole at the tip of the heart. To remove the heart, sever attachments at the base of the heart with one hand while pulling from the hole poked at the tip with the other hand.

Split pelvic bone, clear and protect bung:

- Saw the pelvic bone, or knife through the cartilage if the animal is young enough. Avoid sawing into the bung area.
- Grab a newspaper bag–sized plastic bag and with one hand inside this bag, grab the bung of the animal and cut around it to free it from the interior of the pelvis. Once freed, fold the plastic bag over the first eight inches of bung and tie into place with a

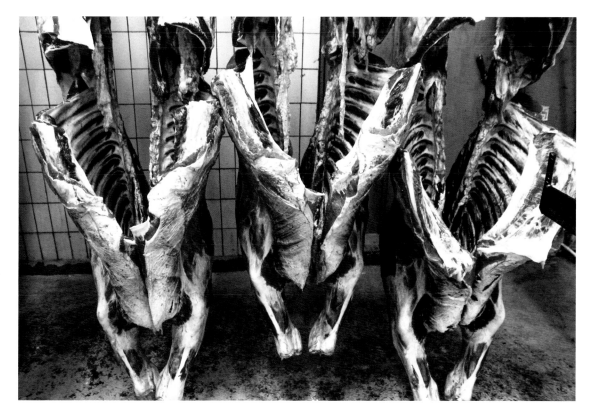

cotton string. This will contain the feces and prevent contaminating the carcass during the gutting process.

Skin and remove oxtail:

- Draw a line down the underside of the tail hide and peel hide away from oxtail.
- Remove the oxtail at the first caudal vertebra.

Hoist gambrel to prepare for gutting. Remove guts:

- Finish hoisting to a position where the neck and foreshanks just clear the ground.
- Cut at the midline of the belly while taking care not to puncture the gut with your knife.

- Pull at the bung bag and guide it down toward the ground, severing any connections near kidney fat that attach the bung to the cavity. Do not cut into the bung or colon.
- As the gut drops, block the gut with your knees to control its descent as you work with your hands.
- As the bung passes the kidneys and hanger, reach in and attempt to puncture the white membrane that extends from the diaphragm. By doing so, there will be a pressure release that will minimize chances of tearing open the gut contents due to a heavy gut and forces of gravity.

- Remove the hanger. Remove the liver. Cut directly along the inside of the spinal column to separate the lungs, and free the remainder of the stomach attachments from the inner walls of the sternum, rib cage, and neck area.

Splitting the carcass:

- It may be helpful to cut a line for yourself to follow if splitting from the exterior of the animal.
- Prepare the neck and upper shoulder area by cutting through the neck meat to expose the vertebrae. Begin splitting from the sacral vertebrae (the tail area) and move down the carcass, lifting and readjusting the saw as needed if you get off track. The goal is to split directly in the middle of the vertebrae and spinous processes (feather bones).
- When using a Sawzall, because of its shorter saw blade length, it is common to split from the interior side of the carcass while standing in the same position as you would when gutting the animal.

Trim, hose, and bacterial intervention:

- Trim any areas of the carcass that may have been smeared with contaminants such as hair, dirt, feces, ingesta, etc. Check and recheck the areas of the neck, the bung, the shanks, and the midline of the belly.
- Hose with pressurized water.
- Use (optional) the spray with a mist of diluted vinegar water for a more sterilized clean up.

Quartering:

- First, find the thirteenth rib by standing either on the interior or exterior side of the hanging carcass. Visually you may be able to see this last rib, which is closest to the flank primal. If there is excessive fat cover, you will have to feel for it with your hand. With a boning knife, cut in between the twelfth and thirteenth rib. Hug the twelfth rib and cut outward through the flank but leave a few inches of attached tissue. Complete your cut in the opposite direction by hugging the twelfth rib and cutting through the loin muscle (longissimus). Direct your cut though the longissimus muscle so that your line of cut ends in the middle of the vertebra, which is the eighth vertebra counted from the juncture of the lumbar and sacral vertebra.
- Attach a hook or rope in the front quarter that will be strong enough to hold the entire weight of the front quarter without slipping out or breaking. Attach this hook between the ribs, ideally between the tenth and eleventh rib, four to six inches away from the rib loin muscles.
- Proceed to saw in the middle of the eight vertebrae (as counted from the sacral vertebrae) to separate the forequarter from the hindquarter.
- Cut the remaining few inches of attachment at the flank.

Cooling and aging considerations:

- For optimal aging, bring the carcass down to a temperature below 38°F and above 32°F in as short of an amount of time as possible.

- Allow to age at these temperatures from a hanging position for a minimum of fourteen days. Beef carcasses can be aged for anywhere from two to six weeks before fabricating. Subprimals can be aged for even longer than that. There is no one-size-fit-all optimal time for aging. Some fatty beef can benefit from longer aging. Some leaner beef will not hold up well to aging and will need to be cut sooner.
- The quality of the refrigeration chamber is of utmost importance. If detrimental bacteria are introduced into the cooler, those bacteria may proliferate if it is not outcompeted by the beneficial bacteria. This is why the slaughterman must trim off all of the dirt and feces, etc., from the carcass prior to refrigerating.
- Clean carcasses will lend to a clean refrigerator.
- Maintain proper circulation of air with the use of stationary fans.
- Keep your "rapid cooling" chamber separate from your "long duration" cooling chamber.
- Move the carcass from the "rapid cooling" hot box to the "long duration" cooler once the carcass is down to temperature.

Fabricating prep, tools, and considerations:

- One 5- to 6-inch boning knife for boning and trimming.

- One 8- to 12-inch steak knife for cutting steaks and trimming.
- Band saw, handheld saw, or other sawing tool.
- Clean table.

Fabrication methods:

- It is of no matter whether we break the carcass into primals from a hanging position or on a table. In either case the purpose is served.
- There are many and varied carcass-breaking strategies and techniques. The following are a few suggested strategies.

Hindquarter:
Remove flank:

- The flank will attach at the trip-tip area to the hind leg (round). Without cutting into the trip-tip, begin separating the flank from the round. At the protrusion of the hip bone, start to create a straight cut parallel to the vertebrae, four to five inches in distance from the erector spinae muscles. Continue this straight cut to the thirteenth rib. Saw the thirteenth rib to remove the entire flank primal.
- From the flank primal, the flank steak (rectus abdominus) and the sirloin flap steak (bavette, internal obliques) can be extracted.

Remove kidney fat:

- To remove the suet, or kidney fat, the seam between the tenderloin and the suet must be found. Take care not to cut into the tenderloin muscle.

Peel butt of tenderloin and remove short loin:

- Starting at the ball and socket portion of the aitchbone, cut across the extreme top of the tenderloin (psoas major) in order to locate the diameter and seam of the muscle. Follow this seam as you peel the butt of the tenderloin down. You will encounter the surface of the pelvis. Scrape, knife, and peel the butt of the tenderloin away from the pelvis bone until you reach the bottom of the hip bone.
- Knife in between the last lumbar vertebra and first sacral vertebra. Cut, snap, or saw to remove the short loin from sirloin/round.
- Alternatively, saw through the middle of the second-to-last lumbar vertebra. Finish the straight cut with a knife.

Remove tri-tip and sirloin:

- Peel the tri-tip partially from the sirloin tip. Once you reach near the bottom of the sirloin tip, straight cut across. Straight cut below the femur joint, aiming for a point two to three inches above the last sacral vertebrae (tail).

- Peel the sirloin from the aitchbone.
- Separate the tri-tip from the sirloin.
- Crosscut the sirloin against the grain for boneless sirloin steaks.

Remove oyster steak and aitchbone:
- Scoop out the oyster steak with your knife.
- Remove the aitchbone by tracing with your knife and staying as close to the bone as possible.

Remove top-round:
- Beginning at the sartorius muscle, seam out the top round muscle.
- Remove the top round cap (gracilis) and prepare for a steak or trim.
- Denude top round and prepare for London broil, steaks, or roast.

Remove sirloin tip:
- Remove sirloin tip by peeling from the femur bone.

- Remove kneecap and clean outer membrane to prepare for steaks or roast.

Remove gooseneck:
- The gooseneck is the combined heel, eye of round, and bottom round.
- Bottom and eye of round can be cleaned and prepared for roasts and steaks, cut thin for stir-fry, or cubed into stew meat. These muscles are exceptionally lean.

Saw or debone shank:
- Shanks are commonly crosscut to create a version of osso buco.
- Alternatively, they can be boned out for grind.

Bones:
- Femur, humerus, and tibia are the bones that contain the most marrow. By sawing across these bones, it will be easier to access the marrow for further processing.

- Spinal column bones, when sawed into manageable pieces, will be ideal for creating a very gelatinous bone stock.

Forequarter:
Separate rib primal from chuck primal:

- Commonly this is done by knife cutting and then sawing between the fifth and sixth vertebrae.

Decide on fabrication for rib primal:

- The rib roast will need to be sawed from the rib plate area. Commonly this saw mark will occur three to four inches from the muscles of the ribeye. This will be a straight cut that travels parallel to the direction of the spine.
- The rib plate can be boned out for grind.
- Alternatively, the rib plate can be cut into English-style short ribs or flanked-style short ribs.
- The rib roast can be deboned for boneless ribeye steaks. It can be deboned and tied for a boneless rib roastif. It can be partially deboned and have the ribs tied back on for a bone-in standing rib-roast. There are many options.

Decide on fabrication for chuck primal:

- There are many tender cuts in the rotator cuff area of the chuck, yet the removal of these cuts can be fairly advanced, and a novice should not attempt this. Instead, a novice should start by preparing a square-cut chuck and creating seven-bone roasts. These old-school pot roasts are amazing. They have somewhat gone out of vogue with the advent of the flat-iron steak and the popularization of seam butchery. Yet they should not be forgotten and make an incredible slow and low roast.

Remove brisket and fore-shank:

- Knife and saw a straight cut beginning at the tip of the sternum, passing two to three inches above the elbow joint, and finishing at the fifth rib. Make sure to leave a good-sized brisket.

- Remove the foreshank from the brisket by following the seam. Debone the shank for trim, or crosscut into an osso buco style preparation.
- Trim the heavy fat off the brisket. The amount of fat trimmed will depend on the culinary preparation the chef will be deciding upon.

Remove shoulder clod:

- Locate the edge of the scapula at the fifth rib. Locate the GH joint by noticing a protruding hard spot where the scapula and the humerus intersect. Knife and then saw a straight cut leading from the edge of the scapula and traveling across the GH joint. Continue knifing and sawing as you completely separate the clod section.
- Locate the humerus bone. Remove this bone. The less meaty side of this bone can go to trim. The meatier side is the crossrib section. Square up this section; clean any excessive fat and fascia to create one large or two small crossrib roasts. Alternatively, the crossrib can be completely denuded and cut against the grain into boneless "ranch" steaks.

Fabricate chuck roasts:

- The remaining portion of the chuck houses the upper thoracic vertebrae and the scapula or shoulder blade bone. There are a range of tender and tough muscles in this area that will do well when cooked slow and low.
- Blade roasts and seven-bone roasts can be cut in various thicknesses, beginning at the

fifth rib. Commonly, these are cut two to three inches in thickness by straight cutting and sawing at intervals parallel to the face cut near the fifth rib.
- Continue creating blade roasts until the vertebrae begin to curve upward along the neck.

Decide on neck fabrication:

- The shoulder will flow into the neck area. The neck can be deboned for a boneless neck roast, used for trim, or portioned into braising chops or bone-in neck roast.

Trim and sausages considerations:

- In many situations, beef trim will be utilized for grind. It is a good idea to decide on how much or how little ground beef, and therefore trim, will be desired.
- The areas of the flanks, shanks, breast, neck, and shoulders all are commonly used for ground beef. When the demand for trim/grind is not present, many of these areas can be left as roasts, braising cuts, or cubed for stew meat.

Beef:
Recipes & Wine Pairings

The following recipes are graciously provided by the Washington State Beef Commission.

The Washington State Beef Commission is a state agency funded by a portion of all cattle sold in Washington State per the Federal Beef Promotion and Research Act & Order and Washington State RCW 16.67. The purpose of the commission is to fund beef promotion, research, and consumer education activities supporting Washington State's multibillion-dollar beef industry.

Accompanying each recipe are suggested wine pairings provided by Clos Du Val and Mark Ryan Winery.

John and Henrietta Goelet founded Clos Du Val in 1972. A descendent of Bordeaux's famed wine merchant Barton & Gustier, John had a vision of producing Cabernet Sauvignon that would rival the world's best. Today, Clos Du Val remains focused on the growing and production of the world's finest wines, specializing in creating small-batch, single vineyard, estate wines from their historic Stags Leap District vineyards in Napa, California.

Mark Ryan McNeilly founded Mark Ryan Winery in 1999 with the goal of making the best wines in Washington State. Largely self-taught, Mark honed the craft of winemaking through rigorous study and the welcomed advice of some of the area's most experienced producers. Today, Mark Ryan Winery has grown in size, earned acclaim from wine-lovers and critics alike, and garnered respect from the state's elite producers. The goal, however, remains the same: Make delicious wines that represent the vineyard from which they come, making every vintage better than the last.

Mark Ryan
WINERY
LONG HAUL
Merlot
WASHINGTON STATE
APPELLATION
COLUMBIA VALLEY
80% MERLOT, 9% CABERNET SAUVIGNON,
8% CABERNET FRANC, 3% PETIT VERDOT

Mark Ryan
WINERY
DEAD HORSE
Cabernet Sauvignon
WASHINGTON STATE
RED MOUNTAIN
2016

Balsamic Onion Mocha Flank Steak

Serves 4

Ground espresso and cocoa powder are the secret ingredients in this dish. Flank steak never tasted so good!

1 (about 1½- to 2-pound) flank steak
1 cup light balsamic vinaigrette dressing (such as Newman's Own), divided
1 tablespoon unsweetened cocoa powder
1 tablespoon ground espresso coffee
½ teaspoon ground black pepper
1 medium onion, peeled and chopped

Pat the flank steak dry with paper towel.

In a small bowl, combine ⅓ cup of the vinaigrette, cocoa, coffee, and pepper. Place the flank steak and marinade in a large food-safe plastic bag and gently toss to coat. Close the bag securely and let marinate in the refrigerator 6 hours or as long as overnight, turning occasionally.

Remove the steak from the bag, discarding the marinade. Place the steak on the rack of a broiler pan so the surface of the meat is 2 to 3 inches from the heat source. Broil 13 to 18 minutes for medium rare (145°F) to medium (160°F) doneness, turning once.

Meanwhile, cook the onion and remaining ⅔ cup balsamic vinaigrette in a medium saucepan over medium heat, uncovered, 8 to 10 minutes or until the onion is tender. Remove from heat.

To serve, carve the steak diagonally across the grain into thin slices. Top with the onion and serve immediately.

WINE SUGGESTION:

Clos Du Val Estate SVS Merlot

SVS stands for special vineyard selection. This was a term coined by Clos Du Val's winemaker Ted Henry as he was creating a wine made with very carefully selected fruit from certain estate vineyards. The light and earthy qualities in this dish will pair beautifully with this robust and bold Merlot. Notes of blueberry tart and baking spices immediately fill the palate, leading to a chalky, long finish.

Beef Brisket with Savory Carrots and Dried Plums

Serves 4 to 6

This beef brisket is as flavorful as can be. Carrots and dried plums make for the perfect autumn accompaniment to this roast.

2 tablespoons olive oil
1 (2½- to 3-pound) boneless
   beef brisket
½ cup chopped onion
1 cup water
5 cups sliced or baby carrots
¼ cup packed brown sugar
1 tablespoon fresh lemon juice
1 teaspoon salt
½ teaspoon ground cinnamon
½ teaspoon black pepper
8 ounces pitted prunes

Pat the brisket dry.

Heat the oil in a stockpot over medium heat until hot. Place the brisket in the stockpot and brown evenly. Remove the brisket and pour off the drippings, if necessary.

Add the onion to the stockpot. Cook and stir for 5 minutes or until the onion is tender. Add the water and cook 1 to 2 minutes or until the browned bits attached to the pot are dissolved. Return the brisket and bring to a boil. Reduce the heat, cover tightly, and simmer for 2¾ to 3¼ hours. Add the carrots, brown sugar, lemon juice, salt, cinnamon, pepper, and prunes. Continue cooking, covered, for 30 minutes or until the brisket is fork-tender. Remove the brisket, carrots, and prunes, and keep warm.

Bring the cooking liquid to a boil. Cook, uncovered, over medium-high heat 5 to 7 minutes or until the liquid is reduced to 1 cup. Trim the fat from the brisket, carve diagonally across the grain, and serve with the carrots, prunes, and sauce.

WINE SUGGESTION:

Mark Ryan Winery, The Shift Syrah, Washington State, Syrah

The Shift Syrah highlights a style that embraces pure fruit and soft smooth tannins. This classic partnership of Syrah Grenache and Mourvedre, The Shift is a great expression of these two varietals. Bold, dark flavors mingle with hints of bright red fruit from the Mourvedre. As always, the texture is superb, with softness and depth through the finish.

Beef Osso Buco with Gremolata

Serves 4

2–3 pounds beef shank crosscuts, cut 1 to 1½ inches thick

2 tablespoons all-purpose flour

1 tablespoon vegetable oil, divided

1 cup finely chopped onion

½ cup finely chopped carrot

½ cup finely chopped celery

1 cup dry white wine

1 (14½-ounce) can diced tomatoes

½ cup packed fresh Italian parsley

1 tablespoon grated orange peel

2 cloves garlic, peeled

Salt and pepper, to taste

Lightly coat the beef shank crosscuts with flour. Heat half of the oil in a stockpot over medium heat until hot. Brown half of the beef shanks on all sides. Remove from stockpot. Repeat with the remaining oil and shanks. Pour off the drippings and season with salt and pepper, as desired.

Add the onion, carrot, and celery to the stockpot. Cook and stir 3 to 5 minutes or until the vegetables are crisp-tender. Add the wine. Cook and stir 2 to 3 minutes or until the browned bits attached to stockpot are dissolved. Cook an additional 5 to 8 minutes or until most of the liquid has evaporated, stirring occasionally. Stir in the tomatoes.

Return the beef shank crosscuts to the stockpot. Bring to a boil. Reduce heat, cover tightly, and simmer 2 to 3 hours or until beef is fork-tender.

Meanwhile, prepare the gremolata by placing the parsley, orange peel, and garlic in a food processor or blender container. Cover and process until finely chopped, stopping to scrape the sides of the container as needed. Cover and refrigerate until ready to use.

Remove the beef shank crosscuts. Cut the beef from the bones and set aside. Skim the fat from the cooking liquid. Bring the cooking liquid to a boil and cook 5 to 10 minutes or until reduced to 2 cups. Season with salt and pepper, as desired. Return the beef to the cooking liquid.

Serve with the gremolata sauce and a side of creamy polenta (optional).

WINE SUGGESTION:

Mark Ryan Winery, Long Haul, Washington State, Merlot

The Long Haul is composed primarily of Merlot from Yakima Valley's Red Willow Vineyard. With an average vine age of twenty-five years, and planted on ancient soils, Red Willow Merlot offers a savory aromatic profile and a complex depth and intensity on the palate. Every effort is made to treat the wine as gently as possible.

Beef Sirloin Pasta Portobello

Serves 4

Savor the amazing combination of beef sirloin and mushrooms in this simple pasta dish with fresh bell peppers, basil, and Romano cheese.

8 ounces uncooked linguine or angel-hair pasta

1¼ pounds boneless top sirloin, cut 1 inch thick

2–3 tablespoons olive oil, divided

2 large cloves garlic, peeled and crushed

½ teaspoon salt

½ teaspoon pepper

8 ounces portobello mushroom caps, cut in half, then cut crosswise into ¼-inch-thick slices

1 medium red, yellow, or green bell pepper, cut into ⅛-inch thick strips

2 tablespoons thinly sliced fresh basil leaves

⅓ cup freshly grated Romano cheese, for garnish

Fresh basil sprigs and bell pepper rings, for garnish

Cook the pasta according to package directions. Drain and keep warm until ready to serve.

Meanwhile, trim the fat from the beef, then cut the steak lengthwise in half and then crosswise into ⅛-inch-thick strips.

In a wok or large nonstick skillet, heat 1 to 2 tablespoons of oil over medium-high heat until hot. Add the beef and garlic, half at a time, and stir-fry 1 to 2 minutes, or until the outside surface is no longer pink. Remove from the pan with a slotted spoon. Season with salt and pepper and keep warm.

In the same pan, heat 1 tablespoon oil until hot. Add the mushrooms and bell pepper strips. Stir-fry 3 to 4 minutes or until mushrooms are tender. Remove from heat and return the beef to the pan. Add the sliced basil and toss.

To serve, place the pasta on a large deep platter and arrange the beef mixture on top. Sprinkle the cheese over the beef and pasta. Garnish with the basil sprigs and bell pepper rings. Serve immediately.

WINE SUGGESTION:

Mark Ryan Winery, Little Sister, Washington State, Merlot

The combination of two world-class vineyards and an exceptional growing season provides Mark Ryan Winery with the opportunity to produce remarkable Merlots. This particular wine is lightly pressed to barrel, where it finishes primary and malolactic fermentation and is aged for twenty-one months in 44 percent new French oak. The wine was racked twice prior to being bottled.

Beef Tenderloin with Roasted Cauliflower Steak

Serves 4

Two "steaks" in one recipe! Try these juicy tenderloin steaks with roasted cauliflower cut into "steak" portions.

1 large head cauliflower

2 tablespoons olive oil

1 teaspoon salt

1 teaspoon black pepper

½ teaspoon dried minced onion

½ teaspoon granulated garlic

4 beef tenderloin (filet mignon) steaks, cut ¾-inch thick (about 4 ounces each)

2 tablespoons prepared creamy horseradish sauce

Preheat the oven to 400°F.

Trim the leaves from the cauliflower, leaving the stem intact. Cut the cauliflower vertically from the top through the stem. Cut each half into two ¾-inch slices, saving any florets or large pieces that remain. Place the cauliflower on a sheet pan and drizzle both sides with olive oil.

In a small bowl, combine the salt, pepper, onion, and garlic. Sprinkle some of the rub over both sides of the cauliflower slices, reserving the remaining rub for the steaks. Transfer to the oven and bake 40 minutes, or until the cauliflower is tender. Note: To reduce roasting time, cauliflower florets may be substituted for the slices and roasted 25 to 35 minutes.

Next, heat a medium ovenproof skillet over medium-high heat until hot. Coat the steaks on both sides with the remaining rub. Brown the steaks on both sides in the skillet. Transfer the skillet to the oven and cook about 15 minutes for medium rare (internal temperature of 145°F).

Remove the steaks and carve into thin slices. Serve the steak slices atop the cauliflower steaks. Drizzle with the prepared horseradish sauce and serve.

WINE SUGGESTION:

Mark Ryan Winery, Dead Horse, Washington State, Cabernet Sauvignon

Washington's finest Cabernet Sauvignon sites provided fruit for the Dead Horse. Every effort is made to treat the wine as gently as possible. The must is never put through pumps and gentle punch-downs occur twice per day. The wine is lightly pressed to barrel, where it finishes primary and malolactic fermentation, and is aged for twenty-one months in 74 percent new French oak. The wine was racked twice prior to being bottled.

Walnut-Crusted Roast with Blue Cheese Mashed Potatoes

Serves 4 to 6

1 (2- to 3-pound) beef eye of round roast
½ cup finely chopped walnuts
3 tablespoons finely chopped green onions
½ teaspoon black pepper
4 cups prepared mashed potatoes, warmed
½ cup crumbled blue cheese

Preheat the oven to 325°F.

Pat the roast dry.

In a small bowl, combine the walnuts, onion, and black pepper. Press evenly onto all surfaces of the roast.

Place the roast on a rack in a shallow roasting pan. Insert an ovenproof meat thermometer so the tip is centered in the thickest part of the roast, not resting in fat or touching bone. Do not add water and do not cover. Roast in the preheated oven 1¼ to 1½ hours for medium rare. Do not overcook.

Remove the roast when the meat thermometer registers 135°F. Transfer the roast to a carving board. Tent loosely with aluminum foil and let stand 15 to 20 minutes. (Note: Temperature will continue to rise about 10°F to reach 145°F for medium rare.)

Meanwhile, combine the mashed potatoes and cheese in a large bowl. Keep warm.

To serve, carve the roast into thin slices, season with salt and pepper, as desired, and serve with the Blue Cheese Mashed Potatoes.

WINE SUGGESTION:

Clos Du Val, Estate Three Graces

The pinnacle of Clos Du Val's portfolio, the Three Graces red blend is named after the daughters of Zeus, who were said to represent elegance, vibrancy, and cheer—the very things Clos Du Val believes wine imparts to life. The owners of Clos Du Val, the Goelet family, own a copper statue of the goddesses, which is now displayed in the Boston Museum of Fine Arts. The Three Graces also serve as the logo for the winery. This wine is big, full, and complex—with each vintage being one of a kind. The bold fruit and silky tannins with hold up well to a roast and blue cheese mashed potatoes.

Rustic Beef Caldo

Serves 4

Caldo = Soup. This recipe = delicious! Chock-full of tender beef, vegetables, and a rich broth, this will warm up any cold day.

1 tablespoon vegetable oil

3 pounds beef shanks crosscut, cut 1 to 1½ inches thick

2 cups water

14–14½ ounces beef broth (Better Than Bouillon)

2 tablespoons chopped fresh cilantro

4 garlic cloves, peeled and minced

2 teaspoons salt

2 teaspoons black pepper

½ teaspoon ground cumin

5 cups coarsely chopped cabbage

2 medium ears corn, husked, cut into 3 pieces each

½ pound small red-skinned potatoes, cut in half or left whole if small

1 large onion, peeled and cut into 1-inch pieces

2 medium carrots, cut into 1-inch pieces

2 medium zucchini or Mexican zucchini, cut into 1-inch pieces

2 medium tomatoes, cut into 1-inch pieces

1 lime, cut into wedges, optional

Heat the oil in a stockpot over medium heat until hot. Brown the beef shanks, in batches, on all sides. Pour off the drippings.

Return the beef shanks to the stockpot. Add the water, broth, cilantro, garlic, salt, pepper, and cumin. Bring to a boil. Reduce the heat, cover tightly, and simmer for 1¾ to 2 hours or until the beef is fork-tender.

Add the cabbage, corn, potatoes, onion, and carrots to the stockpot. Return to a simmer. Reduce the heat, cover tightly, and simmer for 20 minutes. Add the zucchini and tomatoes; simmer, covered, 10 to 15 minutes or until the vegetables are tender.

Remove from the heat and garnish with lime wedges, if desired.

WINE SUGGESTION:

Clos Du Val, Estate Cabernet Sauvignon

Clos Du Val was founded in 1972 on a dream to create the best Cabernet in the world. Their inaugural wine, the 1972 Clos Du Val Cabernet Sauvignon, was part of the group that topped French wines in the legendary 1976 Judgment of Paris blind tasting. Ten years later, their Cabernet Sauvignon took first place in the Judgment of Paris rematch. Clos Du Val's Estate Cabernet is brimming with classic characteristics of cassis, bramble fruit, and blueberry. A long, smooth finish make this the perfect wine to pair with a savory pot roast.

Beef Tortilla Soup

Serves 4 to 6

1 (2½- to 3½-pound) beef brisket flat half

1 tablespoon olive oil

2 cups chopped onions

2 tablespoons ground cumin

2 tablespoons minced garlic

14–14½ ounces unsalted beef broth (Better Than Bouillon)

1 (16-ounce) jar Herdez Salsa Casera

1 (14½-ounce) can no-salt-added diced tomatoes

2 corn tortillas

2 cups frozen corn

2 tablespoons hot pepper sauce

¼ cup chopped fresh cilantro leaves

16 sprigs fresh cilantro, for garnish

1 ripe avocado, peeled, pitted, and thinly sliced, for garnish

½ cup finely shredded reduced-fat cheddar cheese, for garnish

Pat the brisket dry.

Heat the oil in a stockpot over medium heat until hot. Place the brisket in the stockpot and brown evenly. Remove the brisket and season with salt and pepper, as desired. Set aside.

Add the onions, cumin, and garlic to the stockpot. Cook and stir 3 to 5 minutes or until the onions are crisp-tender. Return the brisket, fat-side up, to the stockpot. Add the broth, salsa, and tomatoes. Bring to a boil, then reduce heat. Cover tightly and simmer 2½ to 3 hours or until the brisket is fork-tender.

Next, cut the corn tortillas in half, then crosswise into ¼-inch-wide strips. Place the strips in a single layer on a baking sheet. Spray the tortilla strips lightly with nonstick cooking spray. Bake 4 to 8 minutes at 400°F or until crisp. Set aside to cool.

Remove the brisket. Skim the fat from the cooking liquid, then trim the fat from the brisket. Cut into 4 to 6 pieces; shred with 2 forks. Return the beef to the stockpot. Add the corn and pepper sauce. Cook 20 to 25 minutes. Stir in the chopped cilantro. Season with salt and pepper, if desired.

To serve, ladle the soup into bowls. Garnish each serving with the tortilla strips, cilantro sprigs, avocado, and cheese, as desired.

WINE SUGGESTION:

Mark Ryan Winery, Wild Eyed, Washington State, Syrah

The Wild Eyed Syrah is a combination of four premium Syrah clones that give Mark Ryan Winery wonderful blending tools in the cellar. The goal with the Wild Eyed is to offer a glimpse of warmer-climate Washington Syrah. The wine is specifically aged in thick staved 500-liter French oak barrels. Fruit was hand-harvested in September and the wine aged for eighteen months in 44 percent new, 500-liter French oak barrels.

Caribbean Flank Steak with Coconut Rice

Serves 4

1 (8-ounce) can crushed pineapple

¼ cup fresh lime juice

3 tablespoons finely chopped fresh cilantro, divided

1 tablespoon Caribbean jerk seasoning

1 (about 1½-pound) beef flank steak

2 cups water

1 cup uncooked brown rice

3 tablespoons shredded coconut, toasted

2 tablespoons sliced almonds, toasted

Salt, to taste

Drain the pineapple, reserving ¼ cup juice for the marinade while discarding the excess juice. Reserve the crushed pineapple for the Coconut Rice (recipe follows).

In a small bowl, combine the reserved pineapple juice with the lime juice, 2 tablespoons of the cilantro, and the Caribbean jerk seasoning. Place the flank steak and marinade in a large food-safe plastic bag and gently toss to coat. Close the bag securely and let marinate in the refrigerator 6 hours or as long as overnight, turning occasionally.

Next, prepare the Coconut Rice by combining the water and rice in a medium saucepan. Bring to a boil, then reduce the heat. Cover and simmer 35 to 45 minutes or until the rice is tender. Remove from the heat and stir in the crushed pineapple along with the coconut, almonds, and the remaining 1 tablespoon cilantro. Season with salt, as desired.

Preheat an outdoor grill for direct, medium-high heat (page 17).

Remove the steaks from the marinade, discarding marinade. Place the steaks on the prepared grill. Grill, covered, 11 to 16 minutes (or over medium heat on a preheated gas grill for 16 to 21 minutes) for medium rare (145°F) to medium (160°F) doneness, turning occasionally. Season with salt, as desired. Note: To broil, place the steaks on a rack in a broiler pan so the surface of the meat is 2 to 3 inches from the heat source. Broil 13 to 18 minutes for medium rare to medium doneness, turning once.

To serve, carve the steak across the grain into thin slices. Serve with the Coconut Rice.

WINE SUGGESTION:

Clos Du Val Estate Petit Verdot

Petit Verdot is one of the Bordeaux varietals, and, like Cabernet Franc, is often used specifically for blending. This Petit Verdot showcases the beautiful grape in its entirety. With a spicy and flavorful dish like this, you need a big wine to stand up to the jerk seasoning. A wine that can easily take on the job is this Petit Verdot; big, bold, inky, and full of dark fruit.

Garlic and Tri-Pepper-Crusted Beef Roast with Balsamic Sauce

Serves 4 to 6

1 (3- to 4-pound) boneless beef chuck roast

2 tablespoons coarsely crushed or cracked mixed peppercorns (black, white, green, and pink)

4 garlic cloves, peeled and minced

½ teaspoon salt

1 cup balsamic vinegar

¼ cup softened butter

4 teaspoons all-purpose flour

1 cup beef broth (Better Than Bouillon)

¼ teaspoon coarse ground black pepper

Preheat the oven to 350°F.

Pat the roast dry.

In a small bowl, combine the cracked peppercorns, garlic, and salt. Rub and press the mixture evenly onto all surfaces of the roast. Place the roast, fat-side up, on a rack in a shallow roasting pan. Insert an ovenproof meat thermometer so the tip is centered in the thickest part of the roast and not resting in fat or touching bone. Do not add water and do not cover. Roast in the preheated oven for 1¼ to 1¾ hours for medium rare, or 1¾ to 2¼ hours for medium doneness.

Remove the roast when meat thermometer registers 135°F for medium rare, or 150°F for medium. Transfer the roast to a carving board. Tent loosely with aluminum foil and let stand 15 to 20 minutes. (Note: The temperature will continue to rise about 10°F to reach 145°F for medium rare; 160°F for medium.) Skim the fat from the drippings.

Meanwhile, bring the vinegar to a boil in small nonreactive saucepan. Cook over medium heat 20 minutes or until reduced to ¼ cup. Mix the butter and flour in a small bowl until smooth and set aside. Add the broth, reserved drippings, and pepper to the saucepan. Gradually whisk in the butter mixture until smooth. Bring to a boil. Reduce the heat and simmer for 1 minute, stirring constantly. Keep warm.

To serve, carve the roast into slices and serve with the Balsamic Sauce.

WINE SUGGESTION:

Mark Ryan Winery, Board Track Racer, The Chief, Washington State, Cabernet Sauvignon

The Indian Chief motorcycle is one of Mark's favorite bikes. This wine, year in and year out, shows immense complexity, with Cabernet Sauvignon's cedar aromatics and black currant at the forefront. Fresh violets combine with flavors of blackberry and silky vanilla, and subtle chocolate notes. It has a broad finish with a balance of acidity and tannin.

Grilled Skirt Steak Salad with Creamy Avocado Dressing

Serves 4

Marinated grilled skirt steak is placed atop a bed of lettuce, tomato, onion, and green olives and drizzled with homemade avocado dressing for an outstanding salad!

½ cup fresh lime juice, divided

1 tablespoon minced garlic

1 tablespoon chili powder

1½ pounds beef skirt steak, cut into 4- to 6-inch pieces

1 medium avocado, coarsely chopped

¾ cup water

1 peeled garlic clove

½ teaspoon salt

8 cups mixed salad greens

2 large tomatoes, cut into wedges

1 cup thinly sliced red onion

½ cup pimento-stuffed green olives

Salt, to taste

In a small bowl, combine half of the lime juice, garlic, and chili powder. Place the skirt steak and marinade in a large food-safe plastic bag, and gently toss to coat. Close the bag securely and let marinate in the refrigerator 6 hours or as long as overnight, turning occasionally.

Preheat an outdoor grill for direct, medium-high heat (page 17).

Remove the steak from the bag, discarding the marinade.

Place the steaks on the prepared grill. Grill, covered, 7 to 12 minutes (or over medium heat on a preheated gas grill for 8 to 12 minutes) for medium rare (145°F) to medium (160°F) doneness, turning occasionally.

Meanwhile, in a kitchen blender, add the avocado, water, the remaining lime juice, garlic, and salt. Cover and blend until smooth. Cover and set aside.

Carve the steaks diagonally across the grain into thin slices.

To serve, arrange the salad greens on a serving platter. Top with the tomatoes, onion, olives, and steak slices. Season with salt, as desired. Drizzle with half of the creamy avocado dressing while offering the remaining dressing on the side.

WINE SUGGESTION:

Mark Ryan Winery, Lost Soul, Washington State, Syrah

The Lost Soul is a single vineyard representation of Red Willow Syrah and embodies the cooler side of Syrah. It presents a darker, more savory quality. The wine is aged in thick-staved 500-liter French oak barrels. The fruit was hand-harvested in September and aged for an extended period of thirty months in 54 percent new, 500-liter French oak barrels.

Grilled Beef, Summer Squash, and Onion Salad

Serves 2 to 4

Savor the flavors of the summer with this salad topped with grilled beef strip steak, red onions, yellow squash, zucchini, and drizzled with a balsamic glaze.

2 boneless strip steaks, cut 1 inch thick (about 8 ounces each)

¼ cup balsamic vinegar

¼ cup olive oil

1 large garlic clove, peeled and minced

¼ teaspoon salt

⅛ teaspoon black pepper

2 teaspoons garlic-pepper seasoning, divided

1 medium red onion, peeled and cut into 12 wedges

1 medium yellow squash, cut lengthwise in half

1 medium zucchini, cut lengthwise in half

8 cups mixed salad greens

Preheat an outdoor grill for direct, medium-high heat (page 17).

Pat the steaks dry.

Bring the vinegar to a boil in a small nonreactive saucepan. Reduce the heat and simmer for 3 minutes or until reduced by half. Transfer the vinegar to a small bowl and whisk in the oil, garlic, salt, and pepper until blended. Set aside.

Press about 1 teaspoon of garlic-pepper seasoning evenly onto the steaks, reserving some of the seasoning for the vegetables.

Next, soak two 10-inch bamboo skewers in water for about 10 minutes. Remove the skewers and thread only the onion wedges onto the skewers. Brush the skewered onions and cut sides of the squash and zucchini with some oil. Sprinkle with the remaining garlic-pepper seasoning.

Place the steaks on the prepared grill. Grill, covered, 11 to 14 minutes (or over medium heat on a preheated gas grill for 11 to 15 minutes) for medium rare (145°F) to medium (160°F) doneness, turning occasionally.

Grill the squash and zucchini for 8 to 12 minutes (7 to 11 minutes for gas) and the skewered onions 12 to 15 minutes (13 to 16 minutes for gas) or until tender, turning occasionally.

To serve: Cut the squash and zucchini into ¾-inch pieces. Arrange the squash, zucchini, and onions over the salad greens. Carve the steaks into slices, season with salt and pepper, as desired, and arrange over the salad and grilled vegetables. Drizzle the balsamic vinaigrette over the top.

WINE SUGGESTION:

Clos Du Val, Estate SVS, Cabernet Sauvignon

The Cabernet Sauvignon grape varietal is a cross between Cabernet Franc and sauvignon blanc, created sometime during the 1600s. The SVS Cabernet has the structure to stand up to the grilled strip steak—but isn't too big, in which case it would overpower the seasonal vegetables. A true Bordeaux blend, with additions of Cabernet Franc, Merlot, and Petit Verdot, this wine is plush and juicy, making it a very easy sipper.

Harvest Steak and Quinoa Salad

Serves 4

Enjoy a great-tasting harvest salad using skirt steak, quinoa, squash, apple, and almonds.

1 beef skirt steak (about 1 pound), cut into 4 pieces

½ cup low-fat raspberry and walnut salad dressing, divided (Newman's Own)

4 teaspoons stone ground mustard

½ cup uncooked quinoa

2½ cups (about 10 ounces) cubed butternut squash (½-inch cubes)

5 cups spring salad greens

1 large red apple, unpeeled, coarsely chopped

1 cup fat-free crumbled feta cheese (about 4 ounces)

¼ cup sliced almonds, toasted, for garnish

Pat the skirt steak dry.

In a small bowl, combine the salad dressing and mustard. Place the steak and half of the dressing mixture in a large food-safe plastic bag and gently toss to coat. Close the bag securely and let marinate in the refrigerator 6 hours or as long as overnight, turning occasionally. Cover the remaining dressing and refrigerate as well.

Cook the quinoa according to package directions and set aside.

Place the cubed squash in a 2-quart microwave-safe bowl and cover. Microwave on high for 5 minutes. Remove from the microwave, cool, and set aside.

Remove the steak from the bag, discarding the marinade. Place the steak on a rack of a broiler pan so the surface of the meat is 2 to 3 inches from the heat source. Broil 8 to 12 minutes for medium rare (145°F) to medium (160°F) doneness, turning once. Remove from the oven and carve the steak diagonally across the grain into thin slices. Set aside.

In a large bowl, combine the salad greens, squash, apple, cheese, and remaining dressing mixture. Toss to coat. Place the salad on plates. Spoon ½ cup of quinoa in the center of each salad and arrange the beef slices on top. Garnish with toasted almonds.

WINE SUGGESTION:

Clos Du Val, Estate Pinot Noir, Gran Val Vineyard

Gran Val Vineyard is a vineyard location purchased in 1973, a year after Clos Du Val was established as a winery. Carneros was chosen due to the cooler climate, rolling hills, and its similarity to France—where the Clos Du Val Goelet family is from. This southernmost wine growing region in the Napa Valley is ideal for Chardonnay, Pinot Noir, and Merlot. This Pinot is full of bright red cherry flavors and soft, supple tannins on the finish, making it ideal to pair with a summer salad.

Italian Beef and Roasted Vegetable Sandwich

Serves 6

1 (1½- to 2-pound) beef tri-tip roast

1 tablespoon chopped fresh thyme, divided

2 garlic cloves, peeled and minced

2 medium red and/or yellow bell peppers, seeded and cut into strips

2 cups red and/or yellow grape tomatoes, cut in half

2 teaspoons olive oil

¼ teaspoon salt

⅓ cup reduced-fat mayonnaise

2 tablespoons refrigerated basil paste or chopped fresh basil leaves

6 crusty rolls, split and toasted

⅓ cup shredded reduced-fat mozzarella cheese

2 cups baby arugula or spinach

Kosher salt and freshly cracked pepper, to taste

Preheat the oven to 425°F.

Pat the roast dry.

Combine half of the thyme with the garlic and press evenly onto all surfaces of the roast. Place the roast on a rack in a shallow roasting pan. Do not add water and do not cover. Toss the bell pepper strips and tomatoes with oil, and the remaining thyme along with the salt on rimmed baking sheet.

Transfer to the preheated oven and roast for 30 to 40 minutes for medium rare; 40 to 50 minutes for medium doneness. Note: Roast the pepper mixture in the oven with the roast for 30 to 40 minutes or until the vegetables are tender and begin to brown, stirring once.

Remove the roast when an instant-read thermometer registers 135°F for medium rare; 150°F for medium. Transfer the roast to a carving board. Tent loosely with aluminum foil and let stand 10 to 15 minutes. (Note: Temperature will continue to rise about 10°F to reach 145°F for medium rare; 160°F for medium.)

Meanwhile, combine the mayonnaise and basil paste (or leaves). Spread the mixture evenly onto the cut surfaces of the rolls. Carve the roast into thin slices, and season with salt and pepper, as desired. Top each roll evenly with beef, pepper mixture, cheese, and arugula (or spinach). Close sandwiches and serve.

WINE SUGGESTION:

Clos Du Val, Estate Cabernet Franc, Hirondelle Vineyard

Typically seen as a blending grape, Cabernet Franc rarely gets its time to shine as a pure varietal. Coming in at 100 percent Cabernet Franc, this wine showcases just how truly beautiful this grape can be. Dark ruby in color, it radiates brandied cherry and light cocoa aromas. Notes of fresh thyme and tarragon make this the perfect food wine. Big enough to stand up to the beef, but not too heavy to overcome the simplicity of a sandwich.

Herb-Seasoned Rib Roast with Red Wine Pan Sauce

Serves 6

1 well-trimmed beef rib roast
   (2 ribs), small end, chine
   (back) bone removed
   (4 to 6 pounds)
2 tablespoons steak seasoning
   blend (Johnny's Seasoning)
2 teaspoons dried oregano
2 teaspoons dried thyme
Salt, as needed
¼ cup finely chopped red onion
¾ cup dry red wine
About 14 ounces beef broth
   (Better Than Bouillon)
2 tablespoons softened unsalted
   butter
1 tablespoon all-purpose flour

Preheat the oven to 350°F.

Pat the roast dry.

In a small bowl, combine the steak seasoning, oregano, and thyme. Add the salt until there's plenty of mixture for the roast. Press and rub the mixture onto all the surfaces of the roast.

Place the roast, fat-side up, in a shallow roasting pan. Insert an ovenproof meat thermometer so the tip is centered in the thickest part of the roast, not resting in fat or touching bone. Do not add water and do not cover. Roast in the preheated oven 1¾ to 2¼ hours for medium rare; 2¼ to 2¾ hours for medium doneness.

Remove the roast when meat thermometer registers 135°F for medium rare; 145°F for medium. Transfer the roast to a carving board. Tent loosely with aluminum foil and let stand 15 to 20 minutes. (Note: Temperature will continue to rise about 10 to 15°F to reach 145°F for medium rare; 160°F for medium).

Meanwhile, prepare the red wine pan sauce: Skim the fat from the pan drippings, reserving 1 tablespoon. Heat the reserved 1 tablespoon of fat in a 3-quart saucepan over medium heat until hot. Add the onion and cook until tender. Next, place the roasting pan over medium heat, and add the wine. Cook and stir 1 to 2 minutes or until the browned bits attached to the pan are dissolved. Add the wine mixture and broth to the onions in the saucepan. Bring to a boil over medium-high heat. Cook 12 to 13 minutes, or until reduced by about ⅓ (about 1⅓ cups). Reduce the heat to low. Combine the butter and flour in a small bowl until smooth. Whisk into the wine sauce. Cook and stir 1 minute, or until the sauce is thickened.

To serve, carve the roast into slices, season with salt, if desired, and serve with the sauce.

WINE SUGGESTION:

Mark Ryan Winery, Lonely Heart, Washington State, Reserve Cabernet Sauvignon

For the Lonely Heart, Mark Ryan Winery called on Kilpsun Vineyard, one of Washington's finest sites for Cabernet Sauvignon. When working with fruit of such extraordinary quality, Mark Ryan Winery strives to elevate and support its inherent greatness without dominating the profile with heavy-handed winemaking techniques. Their goal is to allow the amazing fruit quality and finished wines to speak for themselves.

Open-Faced Roast Beef and Summer Vegetables

Serves 4

A thinly sliced roast beef sandwich served open-faced with cucumbers and red onion. Easy and delicious!

⅓ cup mild horseradish sauce

2 teaspoons low-fat milk

1 tablespoon chutney (Major Grey's Chutney)

4 large slices dark rye bread

½ medium cucumber, very thinly sliced

½ small red onion, peeled and very thinly sliced

¾ pound thinly sliced roast beef

1 tablespoon snipped chives

In a small bowl, combine the horseradish sauce, milk, and chutney.

Spread one side of each bread slice with 2 teaspoons of the sauce. Top with equal amounts of cucumber, onion, and roast beef. Spoon the remaining sauce evenly over the beef and sprinkle with chives.

WINE SUGGESTION:

Clos Du Val Estate Merlot

While Cabernet Sauvignon was and still remains Clos Du Val's primary focus, the winery has also been growing Merlot since their very first harvest. This red wine is the perfect match for a lighter meal. It's fresh, high in acid, and boasts lively flavors of bright red fruit and spices. The wine's solid tannin structure melts away slowly, leaving a refreshing fruit finish.

Mediterranean Beef Pot Roast

Serves 4 to 6

This is a modern take on the traditional pot roast. Instead of root vegetables and potatoes, this shoulder (chuck) roast simmers in an unexpected yet delicious blend of balsamic vinegar, onions, shallots, and dates.

1 (2½- to 3-pound) boneless beef shoulder roast
¼ cup all-purpose flour
2 tablespoons olive oil
1½ cups water
¼ cup balsamic vinegar
2 small onions, peeled, halved and sliced
4 medium shallots, peeled and sliced
¼ cup chopped dates
½ teaspoon salt
¼–½ teaspoon black pepper

Preheat the oven to 325°F.

Lightly coat the roast with flour. Heat the oil in a Dutch oven over medium heat until hot. Add the roast and brown evenly. Remove the roast and set aside.

Add the water and vinegar to the Dutch oven. Cook and stir until the brown bits attached to the pan are dissolved. Return the roast to the pan. Add the onions, shallots, dates, salt, and pepper. Bring to a boil. Cover tightly and transfer to the preheated oven. Cook for 2¼ to 3¼ hours, or until the roast is fork-tender. Remove the roast and keep warm until ready to serve.

To serve, carve the roast and plate with the vegetables and some of the cooking liquid.

WINE SUGGESTION:

Mark Ryan Winery, The Dissident, Washington State, Red Blend

Some of Washington State's finest vineyards have provided fruit for The Dissident. People sometimes think The Dissident is made up of wines that don't make the cut in the final blends of the Dead Horse and Long Haul, which couldn't be further from the truth. The same vineyards, barrels, and attention to detail that go into crafting The Dissident go into every wine in the Mark Ryan program. The wine is aged for eighteen months in 58 percent new French oak and racked three times and gently fined prior to bottling.

Ribeye Steaks with Fresh Tomato Tapenade

Serves 2

Add a burst of freshness and color to grilled ribeye steaks with a fresh tomato and olive tapenade.

2 bone-in ribeye steaks, cut 1-inch thick (about 12 ounces each)

1 teaspoon salt

2 teaspoons course ground black pepper

1 cup cherry or grape tomatoes, cut in half

1 (2¼-ounce) can sliced ripe olives, drained

¼ cup chopped fresh basil

3 tablespoons shredded Parmesan cheese

Preheat an outdoor grill for direct, medium-high heat (page 17).

Pat the steaks dry.

Press the salt and pepper evenly onto the steaks. Place the steaks on the prepared grill. Grill, covered, 10 to 14 minutes (or over medium heat on a preheated gas grill for 9 to 14 minutes) for medium rare (145°F) to medium (160°F) doneness, turning occasionally. Note: To broil, place the steaks on a rack in a broiler pan so the surface of the meat is 3 to 4 inches from the heat source. Broil 14 to 18 minutes for medium rare to medium doneness, turning once.

Meanwhile, in a small bowl, combine the tomatoes, olives, basil, and cheese.

To serve, plate the steaks and top with the tomato tapenade.

WINE SUGGESTION:

Clos Du Val, Estate Cabernet Sauvignon, Hirondelle Vineyard

Hirondelle is one of Clos Du Val's most prestigious vineyards. Surrounding the estate winery in the Stags Leap District, this single vineyard produces remarkable Bordeaux varietals. Fun fact: The vineyard was named Hirondelle, French for *swallow*, after seeing these birds return to nest at the winery year after year. This 100 percent estate Cabernet Sauvignon is rich in flavors of raspberry jam, toast, espresso, and fresh pastry. Nice acidity but a long velvety finish makes this a delicious complement to a juicy steak.

Butchering
Deer, Elk & Other Wild Game

We are blessed to live at a time in history where hunting for food is a choice rather than a necessity. Then why hunt? Hunter harvested meat, from such animals as deer, elk, wild boar, antelope, and others, is the most humane, clean, and personally rewarding protein choice available. Consider hunting as foraging for meat the same as one would forage for wild mushrooms or ramps. The decision to take another animal's life is not one to take lightly nor is it a choice that everyone will make. Those that hunt respectfully and ethically, however, tap into emotions that can be traced to the dawn of man.

Hunting is a complex subject with many methods, variables, and differing opinions on just about every technique. To give comprehensive instructions on "how to hunt" could fill volumes. What follows are some general practices and principles pertaining primarily to rifle hunting since it is the most common method for first-time hunters.

Hunting and the "perfect" shot:

The goal of ethical hunters is to make a kill that is quick and clean. In practice this becomes a balancing act among three factors: humane kill, shot risk, and meat preservation. A humane kill is one that minimizes pain and suffering for the animal by hitting vital organs, resulting in a quick death. On large mammals, such as deer and antelope, the three primary targets for a humane kill are the head, chest, and neck area. Shot risk is the ability to accurately place your shot on target when considering environmental conditions, distance to target, target size, and the skill level of the shooter. Failure to make

a good shot can result in a miss or, worse, a wounded animal.

Meat preservation is a major consideration of any hunt because harvesting meat is a primary goal. A gunshot is going to result in some meat being damaged, but proper shot placement will minimize the loss. Fortunately, the most humane targets—head, chest, and neck—also result in the least amount of meat being lost.

A successful head shot is the pinnacle of humane kill and meat preservation. Shots that penetrate the cranium create catastrophic damage to the animal's brain and result in an instantaneous kill. There is little meat to be harvested from the head, so this shot also maximizes meat preservation. The shot risk is extremely high, however, because the target is small and often moves unexpectedly. In general, head shots should only be attempted by experienced hunters in good conditions.

A chest shot is the most recommended shot and is utilized by most hunters. It provides a target with a relatively large margin for error and usually damages a minimal amount of meat. The goal of this shot is to hit the animal's heart, which is a small target, but it is surrounded by a larger, vital area—the lungs. To find the aiming point for this shot, visualize a line drawn vertically along the back of the animal's front leg, then visualize a line drawn horizontally across the lower third of the body. The intersection of these two lines is your aiming point. Successfully hitting this area will result in a quick, humane kill.

A neck shot is a third option, but it is a bit controversial among hunters. Shots that hit

near the back of the neck will strike the spinal column and sever major blood vessels, resulting in immediate immobilization and quick death for the animal. Shots that miss these key areas, however, can pass cleanly through the soft neck tissue. Sometimes the animal is immobilized but a second shot is required to finish the kill. Sometimes the animal can run a great distance before succumbing to the wound. Properly done, it is a clean and humane shot, but be aware of the caveats. Shots to the neck do preserve a high amount of meat.

Any shot that is made outside of these three areas will not result in a clean kill. A shot that hits between the rear legs and the ribs is called a "gut shot." They pierce the intestines, which taints the meat from the digestive fluid released. It also results in an animal that will die slowly, often far away from the hunter and not found.

Target Area	Humane	Shot Risk	Meat Preservation
Head	High	High	High
Chest	High	Low	Medium
Neck	Medium	Medium	High
Anywhere Else	Low	Low	Low

After the shot:

A shot is made. What happens next depends on the effect of the shot and the reaction of the animal. The conventional advice is to wait at least 30 minutes after making the shot to approach or track an animal. This gives the animal time to lie down and expire peacefully nearby. Approaching earlier may cause the animal to continue running, making it harder to find. This is good practice but, as with many things, there are always some exceptions depending on circumstances.

Approaching the animal:

Approach any animal slowly that you suspect to be dead. If it's still alive you do not want to spook the animal and cause it to run off. Once close, observe the animal for any signs of life, such as body movement from breathing or closed eyes. A dead animal's eyes are almost always open and always unmoving. A reliable test to ensure the animal is dead is to lightly touch their eye with a stick. No movement or reaction means the animal is dead and can safely be touched.

The next step, before doing anything else, is to properly tag the animal if it's required. Tagging requirements are different in each state, so know the game laws of the area in which you're hunting. If tagging is required then it usually must be completed immediately after the kill and before field dressing.

Field-dressing kit:

For a long time, our ancestors successfully cleaned their kill using only sharpened flint stones. Today, there are many tools available to make field dressing easier, although the most important tool in your kit should be a sharp knife. Once your field-dressing kit is assembled, it is helpful to keep it together in a small bag inside a backpack. When it comes time to clean the animal in the field everything is together and there is no need to search for a missing item with dirty hands.

Tools and equipment:

- Sharp knife, fixed or locking blade.
- Gut hook (optional) for opening abdominal cavity without puncturing intestines.
- Folding or compact saw for cutting open the sternum and pelvis.
- Latex gloves.
- Pen.
- Zip ties.
- Game bag(s).
- 1-gallon sized ziplock bags.
- Cleaning wipes.

Field-dressing basics:

The old saying goes "there's more than one way to skin a cat." This sentiment is true for deer, antelope, and other commonly hunted animals.

The process of removing the entrails after a kill is commonly called "gutting," "cleaning," or "field dressing." There are many different techniques, but the goal of all is to quickly and cleanly remove the entrails from the animal. It is important to remove the entrails as soon as practical after the animal is killed because this allows the meat to begin cooling, which improves its quality.

Move the animal to a relatively level area if possible. If there is any slope, rotate the animal so the head is uphill and tail is downhill. Roll the animal onto its back.

On male animals, start by removing the penis. Lift up on the penis while cutting underneath it along the urethra. Continue cutting until the urethra turns down into the body near

the rear of the pelvis. The penis can then be cut through to remove it from the body or left on to be removed with the intestines.

On female animals, remove udders swollen with milk. Pinch and lift the skin near the front of the udder to provide an area to start an incision. Continue cutting around and under the udder while lifting until it is removed completely. If the udders are not swollen with milk then their removal can be skipped and they can be cut through in a future step.

Some states require proof of sex, such as an udder, to remain on the animal until it arrives at the processing location. Check your local game laws to be sure you are in compliance.

Cut a circle around the anus and vaginal area to a depth of 3 to 4 inches. Start just to the side of the anus then make the cut with a sawing motion while using the pelvic bone as a guide for the circle.

Starting just below the breastbone, make a small, shallow incision just large enough to slip two fingers into. Put the tips of your pointer finger and middle finger into the incision facing up, forming a "V". With your other hand insert the tip of your knife blade between the two fingers with the blade facing up. Moving your hands together, work your way down the belly of your animal using your fingers as a guide to prevent your knife from puncturing the stomach or intestines. Continue the cut down the middle of the pelvis and to the anus.

With your knife, cut through the hide along the breastbone and then up the neck to the base of the jaw.

Cut through the breastbone with your saw to open the chest cavity. Sever the esophagus high up the neck with your knife. The esophagus will look and feel like a semi-rigid plastic hose. Pull downward on the esophagus and it will begin separating from the body. Cut through any connective tissue that is preventing the esophagus from pulling free by hand. With the tissue under tension, often all it takes is just lightly touching it with your knife blade to make it break free. As you continue pulling down, the lungs and heart will be pulled out though the breastbone cut. The heart can be cut free at this time if you wish to harvest it.

The diaphragm separating the heart/lung area from the intestinal area will prevent the innards from being pulled farther until it is cut free. Reach into the chest cavity and cut the diaphragm away by running your knife around the rib cage where it is attached. Once the diaphragm is cut free, the innards can continue to be pulled down and out of the animal. The liver and kidneys can be harvested as the innards are being pulled out.

Skinning and transporting:

Animals small enough to carry can be left whole with the hide on for transportation to a hanging pole, if one is available. Hanging the animal makes the skinning process easier and cleaner.

Before hanging the animal, start by removing the hocks—the skinny, lowest section of the legs. On the rear legs cut a slit down the inside of each leg all the way to the opening created when gutting. At the end of the rear legs, begin peeling away the hide by pulling with one hand and using the knife tip in the other to make small slicing strokes. Pull enough hide away so that the ends of both rear legs and the Achilles tendon are clear. Insert hooks or a gambrel into the slot created by the Achilles tendon to suspend the animal. Continue pulling and gently cutting the hide away, working down the animal until it is completely removed and only the head remains. Use a saw to cut through the neck at the base of the head. The carcass can be gently rinsed with clean water or wiped with a clean rag to remove excess blood and hair. If desired, the carcass can now be lightly sprayed with an organic acid rinse before being encased in a breathable game bag.

Organic Acid Rinse: A solution of 2.5 percent white vinegar to water. This mixture's acidity kills bacteria and other microbes on the surface of the meat without altering the flavor. By killing the microbes, the meat will taste cleaner and can be aged longer before spoilage. Using an organic acid rinse is mandatory practice at many commercial slaughter plants to improve meat safety and quality.

Animals that are too large to be carried whole, such as elk, can be skinned and quartered in the field. On the rear legs find the joint where the hock meets the Achilles tendon. Cut a ring around this joint down to the bone. Cut a slit down the inside of each leg all the way to the opening created when gutting. Repeat this action on the front legs. Starting on one side, begin pulling and cutting the hide away until it is completely away from that side of the animal. Try to keep the inside of the hide clean and laid out flat, because it can work as a blanket to keep the meat off the ground as you work. Remove the front leg and shoulder by cutting along the rib cage between the leg and body. Remove the rear leg by cutting along the pelvic bone and cutting the femur from the hip socket. Remove the loin by cutting along the backbone and down the rib cage until free. Cut away the flank, rib meat, and neck meat for use as trimmings. Reach into the carcass cavity between the pelvic bone and ribs along the backbone to find and remove the tenderloins. Roll the carcass to expose the unworked side and repeat the process. All of the quarters and trimmed meat should be placed into breathable game bags for transportation.

Aging the meat:

It is beneficial to allow the meat to age on the bone for at least forty-eight hours before butchering. It can be aged up to five days unsealed before the outer layer of muscle begins to dry out and a thick skin forms. At this point, the skin would need to be cut away, which increases the difficulty of butchering and reduces overall yield. Aging for up to three weeks can be accomplished by sealing the meat in plastic wrap or vacuum sealing to prevent moisture loss through evaporation.

This aging process allows the meat to work through the natural rigor mortis cycle when all muscles are contracted and "stiff" for about twelve to forty-eight hours. If muscles are cut away from the bone before or during this phase, the meat will not be as tender compared to meat cut away after rigor mortis has passed. After rigor mortis, natural enzymes in the muscles begin to break down connective tissue. This is the start of decomposition; but when the meat is kept between 34 to 39°F, it can be controlled and used to further tenderize the meat.

Butchering:

Staring down at a whole carcass laying on the table in front of you can be intimidating. Take a deep breath, relax, and remind yourself that this is meat cutting, not brain surgery. The worst mistake you can make is ending up with two smaller steaks instead of one large one.

Start by finding a place to work that is well lit and gives you plenty of space. You'll need a sturdy flat surface at least three by five feet, but the more space the better. A long kitchen counter can work. Center islands in a kitchen are great. Tabletops work too, but they are often a bit low and require stooping. If a table is a good height for you, or if it's you have, then it'll work.

Next, you'll need to gather your equipment. A basic equipment list for home butchering includes:

- Plastic tablecloth (for easy clean up)
- Large cutting board
- Boning knife
- Honing steel
- Bone saw or cleaver
- Large bowls/containers
- Hand towels
- Meat grinder
- Scale (optional)
- Plastic wrap
- Butcher paper
- Masking tape
- Felt-tip pen

It is helpful to designate one bowl for unusable scraps and a bowl for trimmings to be used for ground meat. A third container or area on your work surface should be designated for cuts to be packaged.

Spreading a plastic tablecloth, disposable or washable, over your work surface helps to make cleanup easier after processing. Venison fat is not an enjoyable fat to eat, so it should be trimmed and discarded during processing.

Cut away and discard any meat that is bruised, bloodshot or affected by gunshot.

Butchering Deer, Elk & Antelope

The basic process for butchering four-legged mammals is largely the same whether it is cattle, pig, lamb, or any of the many species of deer and antelope. The differences lie in the some of the final meat cuts targeted and the size differences of those cuts. In general, the butchering techniques used for one species translates well to other species.

Front Legs/Shoulders:

Grab the shank of one front leg and pull it away from the body slightly. Cut between the leg and the rib cage, then behind the shoulder blade, pulling the leg away from the body as you cut. There is very little holding the shoulder to the body and it will separate easily. Repeat the process on the other front leg.

Meat from the shoulder is best used for stew or trimmings to grind, so the precision of your cuts is not very critical here. Lay the shoulder on your cutting board with the "inside" facing up and the shank end away from you. Locate the ridge of bone that runs down the shoulder a little off center. Cut along one side of the ridge to begin separating the muscle. Continue cutting under and around the muscle while pulling it back until it is removed completely. Repeat the process on the muscle on the other side of the ridge. Turn the shoulder over. Cut around and under the muscle that covers the top of the shoulder blade to remove it. Trim and discard any surface fat from the meat.

For meat that will be ground later, cut it into pieces small enough to fit through the neck of your grinder. Trim the meat of any large pieces of the thin layer of light gray tissue called silverskin and connective tissue—but it is not necessary for this meat to be completely clear of it. The grinder will make the meat tender as it passes through.

For meat that will be used as stew cubes, cut the muscles into pieces approximately 1x1 inches. Trim the meat of any silverskin and connective tissue. More care should be taken on these pieces to clean it completely of connective tissue.

The foreshank is an often-overlooked piece of meat that is excellent for braising. Cut through the elbow joint to create a whole shank. Alternatively, the shank can be removed by cutting through the bone with a bone saw or cleaver. The shank can be cut farther with a saw or cleaver into two-inch-thick pieces to create osso buco. If you do not want to keep the shank whole, the meat can be cut away from the bone and added to your trimmings for grinding.

Loins:

The loin muscles are commonly called the "backstraps" and are the most prized cut because of their tenderness. There are two loin muscles. Each one runs down the length of the backbone, one per side.

Locate the area where the rear leg muscles stop and the "small of the back" begins. This area can be identified by looking at the muscle seams from the legs, if visible, or by feeling where the mass of the leg muscles stops tapering down to the back. At this place make a deep cut perpendicular to the backbone, cutting through all muscle, including the loin, all the way to the backbone. Next cut along the backbone from the cut you just made all the way up to the neck. This cut should be kept as close as possible to the bone. Gently pull the loin away from the backbone while scraping the bone with your knife edge, working your way up and down the length of the backbone. The action is like rolling the loin back away from the backbone while cutting it free. Take your time to leave as little meat as possible on backbone and down the rib bones. Once the loin muscle is cut free, cut through the thin layer of muscle and connective tissue holding it onto the rib cage. Repeat this process with the loin on the other side.

Pull the layer of fat and dry connective tissue off the top of the loin muscle using your hands. This will reveal the tender muscle underneath covered with silverskin. Removing the silverskin is similar to removing the skin from a fish fillet. Turn the muscle silverskin-side down. Start your knife incision close to the silverskin. Hold the silverskin, then push the knife down along the length of the muscle while pushing the blade lightly down against the cutting board. The result should be a long strip of silverskin relatively free from meat. The process may need to be repeated a couple times as you remove strips of silverskin. Turn the loin over and trim off any remaining pieces of silverskin from the surface.

The loin can be left whole or cut into smaller sections. It is best to leave the sections sized to make one meal, whatever size that may be for your situation.

Rear Legs:

Lay the carcass on one side. Locate where the pelvic bone and the leg muscles meet at the top of the leg. Using the pelvic bone as a guide, begin cutting to separate the muscles from the bone. After cutting as far down as possible from the "top" of the leg, pull the leg up and do the same from the "bottom" side of the leg. Follow the pelvic bone as a guide and quickly you will encounter the hip ball socket. Work the tip of your knife into the socket and around it while moving the leg bone to free the femur. Once done, continue cutting along the pelvic bone from the bottom and top sides of the leg until it is free from the carcass. Flip the carcass over to repeat the process on the other leg.

In general, butchering a whole leg is about separating the major muscles by following and using the natural seams between those muscles. Trace those seams with your knife tip or even your hands to pull the muscles apart.

Start by removing the sirloin muscle. This is located at the top of the leg and will be the heart-shaped muscle that runs from the leg into the small of the back near the loin.

Cut away the Achilles tendon.

Next, the leg bones should be cut out. Lay the leg on the table with the "inside" facing up. Starting at the bottom of the leg, find the bone and cut all the way down to it. Continue the cut all the way to the top of the leg by following the bone and visible muscle seams. Then, using the tip of your knife, cut down around the sides of the bones while pulling the muscles away. Cut down both sides then underneath the bones along the whole length until the bones can be pulled free.

Now separate major muscles by following natural seams. There are three major muscles to target for steaks: top round, eye round, and gooseneck. The rest of the leg meat can be cleaned for use as trimmings or jerky. Start with the "inside" of the leg facing up. The "bottom" should be leg facing left for the left leg and right for the right leg. The large muscle directly in front of you is the top round. It is large and oval-shaped with the muscle fibers running straight along its length. Look inside the leg where the bone was removed to find the natural seam for the top round and cut it away.

The next muscle is the eye round, identified by its long, skinny shape. It looks very similar to a tenderloin and it located next to the top round. Find its seams and cut it away.

Rotate the leg 180 degrees. The large muscle now in front is the gooseneck. Its appearance is similar to the top round except the muscle fibers run diagonally down its length. Follow the seams to cut it away.

The remainder of the leg is good meat that should be cut away, cleaned of connective tissue, and put into the trimmings pile.

Clean any silverskin and connective tissue from the top round, eye round, and gooseneck. These muscles can be left whole or cut into smaller fillets depending on their size and your needs. They are excellent for using in any recipes calling for tender cuts like the loin.

Tenderloins:

The tenderloins are a long skinny muscle that run along the inside of the backbone between the rib cage and the pelvis. Cut down the sides then underneath to pull it free. Clean away the silverskin from the tenderloin.

Neck, Ribs, and Remaining:

After the main cuts have been removed from the carcass, a lot of usable meat is still available. Meat can be cut from the neck, chest, ribs, and any other bones to be used as trimmings for ground meat. There is no need to worry about precise cuts when harvesting this meat. Just be diligent in cutting and scraping away all the meat you can from the bones. Trim away any fat and significant pieces of connective tissue—but some silverskin remaining is okay. Add all this meat to your trimmings bowl.

Bones:

Bones can be used to make a stock or broth.

Grinding:

Grinding your trimmings is an excellent way to maximize your yield from the animal, and it provides you with a versatile cut that can be used in many ways. Meat can be ground using a stand-alone grinder, a stand mixer attachment, or even a hand-cranked grinder.

Meat grinds best when it is very cold because the blades cut it cleaner rather than mash it, which can happen when the meat is warm. Start by placing your grinder tray, auger, plates, and blade into the freezer for at least thirty minutes. Work through your trimmings pile to cut the pieces into one- to two-inch pieces, or at least small enough to fit down the neck of your grinder. Smaller pieces will move down the auger easier. If you have space, lay the meat in a single layer on a tray, then place it into the freezer for one hour or until it is firm but not frozen. If freezer space is not available, then put the meat in your refrigerator until it is well chilled.

Some butchers prefer to add beef fat to game meat for grinding, and some prefer to keep it lean. Added fat can help the meat bind if you intend to use it for hamburger patties or sausage, and adds some moisture to keep it from tasting dry when fully cooked. Your local butcher can likely provide you with some beef fat or trimmings. Alternatively, a fatty cut such as beef brisket can be used to mix in. Add enough fat so that it is 15 to 25 percent of the total weight of the meat. The fat should be cut and chilled with the meat. When grinding, the fat should be mixed in with the meat so they are ground at the same time. If you wish to keep the ground meat lean or you cannot find fat you're comfortable using, then there is absolutely nothing wrong with straight ground venison.

Assemble your chilled grinder according to manufacturer instructions. The plate(s) you use depends on your intended use for the meat. For chili a single grind through a medium sized plate (5/16- or 3/8-inch) provides a coarse grind that holds up well to the slow-cooking process. For hamburger or general use, plan to run the trim through your largest plate (5/16- up to ½-inch) first, then again through your smallest plate (⅛- or 3/16-inch). If in doubt, go with the general-use double-grind option.

Working in small batches, place chilled meat onto the grinder's tray, then use a plunger to feed the meat down the grinder's neck and into the auger. Do not overstuff the neck or use excessive force to push the meat onto the auger. When the meat is fed slowly, the auger will pull the meat through the grinder on its own. Catch the ground meat coming from the grinder in a large bowl or container.

Packaging:

You've worked hard to harvest and butcher this meat, but you can't eat it all at once. Properly packaging your meat to preserve it in the freezer is the critical last step. Minimizing contact with air will prevent freezer burn and preserve the meat longer. It is important to clearly label the package contents, including species, specific cut, and date.

A few options are available for packaging your meat.

Vacuum Sealing: This is the best option but also the most expensive. It requires special equipment and special bags. However, the process removes all air from the bag, which will keep the meat preserved at the highest quality for the longest period of time. Place the meat into the appropriate bag, then follow the vacuum sealer instructions. Label the bag and you're done.

Butcher Paper: This is the most common technique for home butchers because it is inexpensive and requires no special equipment. First, wrap the meat tightly in plastic wrap to create a relatively airtight barrier. Place the wrapped meat in a cut section of butcher paper. Bring two opposite edges of the paper together, then fold the edges together with about a one-inch fold. Continue folding in a "rolling" fashion until you've folded all the way down to the meat. Turn the package over so the folded seam is on the table. Fold a triangle into one end of the paper, then fold the triangle over the top of the package, similar to gift wrapping a present. Repeat the triangle fold on the other side. Tape the triangle folds with masking tape to hold the package together. Label the package.

Bags & Rings: Many butcher supply shops sell food-grade plastic bags that are perfect for packaging ground meat. Fill the bags with ground meat, taking care not to trap large pockets of air. Twist the top closed and secure the top with a twist tie or hog ring. A small scale can be helpful to weigh your packages to keep them a consistent size.

Butchering Wild Boar

Butchering a wild boar can be done exactly the same as for venison. There are a few modifications, however, that should be considered. A wild boar is just a wild pig. Any cuts of domesticated pork that you enjoy can also be fabricated from a wild boar.

Wild boar fat! Venison fat is not enjoyable and should be trimmed away, but a little bit of pig fat can enhance the cuts. Trim the fat when butchering so that about ¼ inch remains.

Belly: If the wild boar is on the larger size, then the belly meat can be used for braised pork belly or even bacon. Make a cut down to the bone about halfway up the rib cage and perpendicular to the rib bones. Continue this cut along the length of the rib cage. Cut the belly meat away from the rib cage by cutting down the rib bones until the belly is freed in one piece. Repeat the process on the other side. The belly meat will be thinner than domesticated pork, so it benefits from being rolled and tied when braising or curing for bacon.

Spareribs: If the wild boar is on the smaller size then the belly meat can be left on the ribs, but they can be cut bone-in for spareribs. Make a cut down to the bone about halfway up the rib cage and perpendicular to the rib bones. Cut through each rib along this line with a saw or a cleaver to create a slab of ribs. Repeat on the other side.

Whole Shoulder: Cut the foreshank away at the shoulder joint. Keep the foreshank whole or cut into osso buco for braising. The scapula can be cut away from the shoulder for a boneless roast or left in for a bone-in roast. Whole wild boar shoulder is excellent braised or smoked.

Venison & Other Wild Game: Recipes and Wine Pairings

The following deer (venison), elk, antelope, and wild boar recipes are graciously provided by Broken Arrow Ranch.

Broken Arrow Ranch is the industry leader in providing pure wild meat to your table. For more than thirty years, the operation has grown, with more mobile meat processing units being sent to harvest on nearly forty unique ranches every year. The team works with wildlife ecologists, ranch owners, and managers to identify overpopulated herds on private land all across the state of Texas, seeking opportunities to use selective harvesting to improve the health of the herd and land. Today, Broken Arrow Ranch's work has expanded beyond just the requirements of taste but has deepened to a focus on purity. Pure food is the best food. It tastes the best, makes our bodies feel the best, and ultimately results in healthier natural ecosystems.

Accompanying each recipe are suggested wine pairings provided by Buty Winery and DeLille Cellars.

DeLille Cellars is a boutique artisan winery located in Woodinville, Washington. The winery is considered a principal influence in establishing Washington State as a premier viticultural region, and has maintained a strong tradition of quality and excellence since its founding in 1992. Today, the winery has a portfolio of over a dozen Bordeaux and Rhône style blends true to the terroir of Washington.

Buty is a family-owned winery located in Walla Walla, Washington, that makes a small portfolio of highly acclaimed wines. Guided by Nina Buty, the Buty team includes legendary consultant Zelma Long and renowned winemaker Chris Dowsett. Buty's wines have earned a reputation for their artistry and for the authenticity that inspires Buty's winemaking approach. Today, Buty's sought-after, limited-production wines are recognized as benchmarks for quality, creativity and value—offering a rare intersection of all three elements.

Bunkhouse Venison Meat Loaf

Serves 4

2 slices fresh whole-wheat bread
   crumbs (about ¾ cup)
1 large egg
½ cup peeled and chopped
   onion
1 garlic clove, peeled and
   minced
½ cup tomato sauce
2 tablespoons chopped fresh
   Italian flat-leaf parsley
1 teaspoon balsamic vinegar
1½ teaspoons Dijon mustard
½ teaspoon dried basil
¼ teaspoon dried thyme
¼ teaspoon dried oregano
½ teaspoon salt
½ teaspoon fresh cracked black
   pepper
1 pound ground venison

Preheat the oven to 350°F.

In a food processor or blender, process the bread until fine crumbs form.

Lightly coat a large baking dish with nonstick cooking spray.

In a large bowl, beat the egg. Add the bread crumbs along with the onion, garlic, tomato sauce, parsley, vinegar, mustard, basil, thyme, oregano, salt, and pepper. Blend all the seasoning ingredients well. Add the venison and blend again. You can use a rubber spatula, but your hands are best to thoroughly mix.

Shape the meat loaf mixture into an oval loaf and place in the prepared pan. Bake for 45 minutes to 1 hour, or until the internal temperature is 150°F. Let stand for 10 minutes before slicing.

WINE SUGGESTION:

DeLille Malbec

The signature characteristics of Malbec are unmistakable, exhibiting leafy black fruits, blueberries, and plum characters with firm, ripe tannins. DeLille Cellars selected Malbec from the renowned Red Willow vineyard in the remote western corner of the Yakima Valley AVA for a small-lot production, and it is the ideal pairing for this hearty dish.

Savory Venison Stew

Serves 4

1 pound venison, cleaned, trimmed, and cut into bite-size pieces

1 tablespoon pickling spice (wrapped in cheesecloth)

1 bay leaf

1 cup coarsely chopped onion

⅛ teaspoon garlic powder

¼ teaspoon cracked black pepper

2 carrots, cut into ½-inch pieces

2 celery stalks, cut into ½-inch pieces

2 red potatoes, cut into ½-inch pieces

2 chicken bouillon cubes

2 cups water

1 teaspoon red wine vinegar

1 (8-ounce) can tomato sauce

Spray a large, deep skillet, stockpot, or Dutch oven with vegetable cooking spray and quickly brown the venison on all sides over medium-high heat. Wrap the pickling spice in cheesecloth and tie with a string. Add the bay leaf, onion, garlic powder, pepper, carrots, celery, potatoes, bouillon, water, vinegar, and tomato sauce. Stir well to incorporate the ingredients.

Reduce the heat to low and slowly simmer for 1½ hours or until the venison is tender. Remove the cheesecloth-wrapped spices before serving.

WINE SUGGESTION:

DeLille Doyenne

The city of Aix-en-Provence is where the first great French wine region was formed, and the art of blending is steeped in history. Doyenne (meaning *wise* or *senior*) is a tribute to this ancient region and respected practice. This blend of Syrah and Cabernet Sauvignon is true to the Doyenne name and the region that inspired its creation, and it pairs well with savory elements.

Venison à la Bourguignonne

Serves 4 to 6

2 cup red wine

1 bay leaf

1 onion, peeled and stuck with 2 cloves

1 garlic clove, peeled and chopped

2 pounds venison, cleaned, trimmed, and cut into bite-size pieces

2 teaspoons fresh thyme

2 teaspoons mustard

1 bunch scallions, chopped

2 teaspoons salt

1 teaspoon fresh cracked black pepper

2½ cups beef stock, or as needed

2 cups peeled pearl onions

8 ounces mushrooms, sliced ¼-inch thick

4 tablespoons cornstarch + ½ cup cold water

6 ounces thick-sliced uncooked bacon

1 sprig fresh Italian flat-leaf parsley, chopped

Prepare the venison by combining, in a large bowl or gallon-sized sealable plastic bag, the red wine, bay leaf, onion, and garlic. Stir to blend and add the venison. Squeeze out the air and seal the bag. Marinate the venison in the refrigerator for up to 3 hours or longer, turning the bag occasionally.

Remove the venison from marinade, reserving the marinade. Allow the meat to remain at room temperature 30 minutes before cooking. Dry venison on paper towels.

Spray a large, deep skillet, stockpot, or Dutch oven with nonstick spray, and brown the venison on all sides over medium-high heat. When brown, add the thyme, mustard, scallions, salt, pepper, and enough beef stock to just cover the meat. Bring to a boil, cover, and simmer gently about 2½ hours or until the meat is tender.

While cooking the venison, fry the bacon, drain, and chop or crumble into small pieces.

Thirty minutes before serving, add the pearl onions and mushrooms to the venison and let cook. Taste and correct the seasonings, if need be. You may want to add more salt, thyme, or mustard. Mix the cornstarch with the water. Slowly pour into the pot, stirring continuously. Remove from heat.

To serve, divide the Venison à la Bourguignonne and garnish with the crumbled bacon and chopped parsley.

WINE SUGGESTION:

DeLille D2

D2 takes its name from the *grand route du vin*, or great wine road that travels through the historic château region of Bordeaux. Always leading with Merlot, D2 is a traditional Bordeaux-style blend sourced from more than fifteen of Washington State's most prestigious vineyards across the Columbia Valley to create the ultimate expression of Washington terroir. The red fruits and moderate structure are a perfect match for this dish.

Venison Kebabs

Serves 4

1 pound venison loin or fillets, cleaned and trimmed

½ cup freshly squeezed orange juice

2 tablespoons rice vinegar

3 tablespoons soy sauce

2 tablespoons peanut oil

1 tablespoon chopped fresh peeled ginger

2 garlic cloves, peeled and thinly sliced

3 scallions, chopped

2 tablespoons chopped fresh cilantro

1 medium onion, peeled and cut into 8 wedges

1 medium red bell pepper, seeded, cored, cut into 8 squares

8 medium mushroom caps

8 cherry tomatoes

4 cups cooked rice

Cube the venison into kebab-size portions. Set aside.

Prepare the marinade by combining, in a large bowl or gallon-sized sealable plastic bag, the orange juice, vinegar, soy sauce, oil, ginger, garlic, scallions, and cilantro. Stir to blend and add the venison cubes. Squeeze out the air and seal the bag. Marinate the venison for up to 2 hours at room temperature or longer in the refrigerator, turning the bag occasionally. Allow the meat to remain at room temperature 30 minutes before cooking. Drain the marinade into a small saucepan and bring to a boil. Remove from the heat and reserve.

Soak four 10-inch bamboo skewers in water for 1 hour.

Next, fill a large bowl or pot with the onion wedges, pepper, and mushrooms. Blanch the vegetables by pouring boiling water over them. Let the vegetables sit in the water for about 10 seconds, then drain and rinse with cold water.

Preheat the oven broiler or preheat an outdoor grill for direct, medium-high heat (see page 17).

Thread the vegetables, including the tomatoes and venison, onto the presoaked skewers, beginning and ending with the onion wedges. Set the skewers on a rack, keeping the rack about 2 to 3 inches from the heat. Broil or grill about 3 minutes per side, basting with the marinade when turning.

Heat the reserved marinade and bring to a boil. Boil for 1 minute. Serve the marinade with the kebabs over cooked rice.

WINE SUGGESTION:

DeLille Signature Syrah

The sandy loam soils and cool nights of the Yakima Valley contribute to crafting a wine with incredible generosity of flavors and spices—qualities that elevate Syrah into an unparalleled category. DeLille chooses to co-ferment this Syrah with 2 percent Viognier, adding another dimension of citrus and floral spices to the bouquet. DeLille Cellars' Signature Syrah pairs well with the smoke of the grill.

Venison Bolognese with Fettucine

Serves 4

This is a savory meat sauce with almost no fat that freezes well.

1 pound ground venison
1 garlic clove, peeled and minced
½ teaspoon vegetable-flavored
   bouillon powder
¾ cup water
1½ cups peeled and chopped onion
1 teaspoon salt
1 (8-ounce) can tomato paste
2 teaspoons Worcestershire sauce
2 teaspoons red wine vinegar
½ teaspoon each Tabasco, basil,
   rosemary, marjoram, fresh
   ground black pepper
1½ teaspoons each oregano, chili
   powder, paprika, sugar
1 bay leaf
1½ cups chopped green pepper
4 ounces fresh mushrooms, sliced
   ¼-inch thick
½ cup fresh Italian flat-leaf parsley,
   minced
1 pound fettuccine (cooked al dente
   according to package directions)

Spray a large pan with nonstick spray and brown the venison and garlic over medium heat. Set aside. Mix the bouillon powder with water and add the onion. Heat in a microwave or on the stove until the onion is soft.

In large, heavy pot, add the salt, tomato paste, Worcestershire sauce, vinegar, Tabasco, basil, rosemary, marjoram, black pepper, oregano, chili powder, paprika, sugar, bay leaf, green pepper, mushrooms, and parsley. Mix well, then add the venison, onion, garlic, and bouillon. Simmer slowly over low heat for 1½ to 2 hours.

Serve over fettucine.

WINE SUGGESTION:

DeLille Harrison Hill

A Bordeaux-style blend from a small, historic vineyard on Snipes Mountain, this wine is labeled after the vineyard's namesake—Harrison Hill. Over the past five decades, the state's second-oldest Cabernet vines have matured gracefully while producing progressively limited yields. This slow, elegant maturation is a compelling expression of what it means to be a terroir-driven wine.

Venison Curry

Serves 6

Axis deer and South Texas (nilgai) antelope are indigenous to India, so this curry recipe is a natural fit.

3 tablespoons vegetable oil
1 cup chopped onion
2 tablespoons ground coriander
1½ teaspoons ground cumin
1 teaspoon ground cardamom
1 teaspoon ground ginger
1 teaspoon ground turmeric
¼ teaspoon cracked black
   pepper
⅛ teaspoon ground red pepper
2 garlic cloves, peeled and
   minced
2 pounds venison, cleaned,
   trimmed, and cut into bite-
   size pieces
1 (14-ounce) can beef broth
1 cup water
1 teaspoon salt
¼ cup plain yogurt
1 teaspoon fresh lemon juice
6 cups cooked rice

In a large sauté pan, heat the oil over medium-high heat until hot. Add the onion and sauté until the soft and golden. Reduce the heat to low, and add the coriander, cumin, cardamom, ginger, turmeric, black pepper, red pepper, and garlic. Stir for 1 minute. Increase the heat to medium and add the venison. Stir frequently until meat is browned. Add the broth, water, and salt. Cover and simmer until the meat is tender, about 2 hours. Uncover and let the sauce thicken, about 20 minutes. Reduce the heat to stop the boiling action and add the yogurt and lemon juice. Stir until well incorporated. Remove from heat.

To serve, place 1 cup of cooked rice on each serving dish. Divide the Venison Curry and spoon over the rice. Arrange the garnishes around the table so each person can add the garnish(s) of their choice.

Garnishes: chutney, chopped scallions, grated hard-boiled eggs, sliced almonds, chopped cucumbers, chopped bananas, coconut, raisins, fresh cilantro, and crumbled bacon pieces.

WINE SUGGESTION:

DeLille Métier

Nowhere is the craft (métier) of blending wine more evident than in DeLille Cellars' Métier, a wine mirrored after traditional Southern Rhône-style blends. This wine combines Old World characteristics with the focus and ripe terroir of Yakima Valley. Red fruits and light structure pair well with this curry dish.

Venison Osso Buco

Serves 4 to 6

Osso buco is an Italian dish that traditionally braises veal shanks. Wild game, like venison, also works thanks to the deep, full flavors it produces. Because braised dishes are often better when allowed to "rest" overnight, make this recipe, if possible, a day in advance. Store overnight in the refrigerator, then reheat when ready to serve. The meat will be more tender with the flavors having had a chance to blend.

4 pounds whole venison shanks
Salt and black pepper, to taste
2 tablespoons butter
2 tablespoons olive oil
1 large onion, peeled and finely chopped
1 large carrot, peeled and finely chopped
2 medium celery stalks, finely chopped
3 large garlic cloves, peeled and finely chopped, divided
¾ cup red wine, preferably Burgundy/Pinot Noir or Zinfandel
1 (14½-ounce) can diced tomatoes, drained (or 2 fresh tomatoes, diced)
4 cups beef broth
2 bay leaves
2 teaspoons fresh thyme
Cornstarch, as needed, optional
3 tablespoons chopped fresh Italian flat-leaf parsley
1 teaspoon finely grated fresh lemon zest

Preheat oven to 325°F.

On the stovetop, heat a large pot over medium-high heat. Season the venison shanks with salt and pepper. Add the butter and olive oil to pot then, working in small batches, add the shanks and brown on both sides. Remove the browned shanks to a platter. Reduce the heat to medium, add the onion, and sauté until it is soft and golden brown (Note: You may have to add a little more butter/olive oil if necessary). Add the carrot and celery and continue to sauté until tender. Add 2 cloves of the garlic and sauté for 1 minute (don't let the garlic burn). Add the red wine and deglaze the pot by scraping up the crusty bits with a wooden spoon or spatula. Add the tomatoes, beef broth, bay leaves, and thyme. Return the venison shanks to the pot along with any accumulated juices.

Cover the pot and cook in the oven until meat is tender, at least 4 to 6 hours. When tender, a fork or knife will easily pierce the meat and separate it. If the meat is not tender, just keep cooking. There is no such thing as tough shanks, just shanks that haven't been cooked long enough. When the shanks are tender, remove them from the pot onto a warm platter. Reduce the remaining pan juices by about half on the stovetop over high heat. If necessary, the sauce can be thickened with a water and cornstarch slurry or *beurre manie* (softened butter and flour mixture). Remove the bay leaves.

Lastly, mix together in a small bowl the parsley, the remaining garlic clove, and lemon zest to create a gremolata.

Serve the venison shanks with the pan sauce and the gremolata. These shanks also go well with "white" creamy sides such as risotto, polenta, bean puree, or simply mashed potatoes.

WINE SUGGESTION:

DeLille Grand Ciel Syrah

At Grand Ciel, DeLille Cellars' Estate Vineyard on Red Mountain, Syrah has taken on a whole new dimension. Traditional methods and modern French clones are combined with the unique climate soils of Red Mountain. The resulting wine is one of great concentration in both fruit and terroir, revealing the meaty, floral, and focused characteristics of Old World Syrah, making this a perfect pairing with gamy venison finished with parsley and lemon zest.

Venison Pot Roast

Serves 6

1 (2- to 4-pound) venison chuck roast or shoulder roast

Salt and black pepper, to taste

2 tablespoons all-purpose flour

1 tablespoon olive oil

2 garlic cloves, peeled and minced

2 tablespoons brown sugar

1 teaspoon mustard

1 tablespoon Worcestershire sauce

¼ cup vinegar or lemon juice

1 (14½-ounce) can tomatoes, with juice

Preheat the oven to 225°F.

Season the roast with salt and pepper and roll in the flour. Add the oil to a large skillet over medium-high heat until hot. Add the roast and brown on all sides.

Place the roast in a casserole dish or Dutch oven, and add the garlic, brown sugar, mustard, Worcestershire sauce, vinegar (or lemon juice), and tomatoes. Cover and cook for 3 to 4 hours, or until the roast is fork-tender.

Remove from heat and serve.

To make a hearty Venison Stew, simply follow the same recipe above, but add to the Dutch oven: 2 pounds of venison, cleaned, trimmed, and cut into bite-size pieces, along with the following ingredients:

3 celery stalks, cut diagonally in 1-inch pieces
½ cup chopped onion
1 tablespoon fresh chopped Italian flat-leaf parsley
8 to 10 small potatoes

WINE SUGGESTION:

DeLille Doyenne

Doyenne is a Red Mountain blend of Syrah and Cabernet Sauvignon, and as always, delivers the best of both varietals. The terroir of Red Mountain is well represented here, with Herbs de Provence and structure throughout, pairing perfectly with pot roast.

Venison-Vegetable Meat Loaf

Serves 8

¾ cup oats
1 small onion, peeled and
   minced
½ teaspoon salt
½ teaspoon cracked black
   pepper
½ teaspoon dried basil
½ cup V8 juice
2 egg whites
1 pound ground venison
1½ cups chopped or shredded
   vegetables (such as carrots,
   zucchini, broccoli, or cooked
   greens)

Preheat the oven to 350°F.

In a large bowl, combine the oats, onion, salt, pepper, basil, and V8. Let stand 5 minutes or until the oats swell slightly. Add the egg whites, venison, and vegetables. Mix well.

In a greased shallow baking pan, add the mixture and shape into a loaf. Bake in the oven for 1 hour. Remove from heat and let sit before serving.

WINE SUGGESTION:

DeLille D2

Leading with Merlot, D2 is dense and vibrant on the palate with a pure fruit core. One of DeLille Cellars' founding wines, it offers elegant tannin and remarkable integration. Incredibly balanced barrel influence and the presence of Cabernet support an extended finish. The red-fruited flavors tie in well with this blended dish.

Venison Stir-Fry

Serves 4

¼ cup dry sherry

1½ tablespoons finely chopped fresh peeled ginger

2 garlic cloves, peeled and finely chopped

1 tablespoon sesame oil

¼ cup soy sauce

1 orange, zested

12 ounces venison, cut into stir-fry strips

1 teaspoon cornstarch

1 tablespoon peanut oil

1 cup broccoli, cut into bite-size pieces

1 medium carrot, peeled and sliced on the bias

1 medium onion, peeled and cut into 8 wedges

½ medium red bell pepper, seeded and cut into pieces

½ medium yellow bell pepper, seeded and cut into pieces

10 mushroom caps, halved

1 cup snow peas, ends trimmed

4 cups cooked rice

¼ cup thinly sliced scallions, for garnish

1 teaspoon toasted sesame seeds, for garnish

Prepare the marinade by combining, in a large bowl or gallon-sized sealable plastic bag, the sherry, ginger, garlic, sesame oil, soy sauce, and orange zest. Stir to blend and add the venison. Squeeze out the air and seal the bag. Marinate the venison for up to 2 hours at room temperature or longer in the refrigerator, turning the bag occasionally. Allow the meat to remain at room temperature 30 minutes before cooking.

Strain the marinade into a measuring cup and add enough water to make ⅓ cup liquid. Add the cornstarch and stir to dissolve.

Heat a nonstick wok or large nonstick skillet over high heat. Add the peanut oil and venison. Stir-fry until the venison loses its red color, about 1 to 2 minutes. Remove the venison with a slotted spoon. Reserve and keep warm.

Stir in the broccoli and carrot. Cover and steam for 1 minute. Uncover and stir in the onion, peppers, and mushrooms. Stir-fry another 3 minutes. Add the snow peas, browned venison, and the reserved marinade/water mixed with cornstarch. Stir continuously until the sauce begins to thicken, about 2 minutes.

To serve, spoon stir-fry the venison and vegetables over cooked rice. Garnish with a sprinkle of scallions and toasted sesame seeds.

WINE SUGGESTION:

DeLille Roussanne

Roussanne is one of the few noble white grapes that can retain natural acidity and crisp structure nurtured under the beloved Red Mountain sun. As a single vineyard wine from the famed Ciel du Cheval vineyard in the Red Mountain AVA, the distinctive mineral complexity pairs well with a little bit of spice.

Elk Hill Country Casserole

Serves 8

1 garlic clove, peeled

2 tablespoons olive oil

1 pound ground elk

1 teaspoon salt

½ teaspoon cracked black
pepper

2 (8-ounce) cans tomato sauce

1 (8-ounce) package small egg
noodles or spaghetti

1 (3-ounce) package cream
cheese, softened

1½ cups sour cream

6 scallions, chopped

½ pound cheddar cheese,
grated

Preheat the oven to 350°F.

In a skillet over medium heat, sauté the garlic in the olive oil. Add the elk to the skillet and brown. Season with salt and pepper and add the tomato sauce. Lower the heat and allow to simmer for 20 minutes.

Meanwhile, cook the noodles according to package directions. In a separate bowl, combine cream cheese, sour cream, and scallions. Place the noodles in a greased 13 x 9-inch casserole dish. Top with cream cheese mixture and then the meat mixture. Sprinkle cheddar cheese on top. Bake, uncovered, about 30 minutes, or until hot and bubbly.

WINE SUGGESTION:

2015 Buty Rediviva of the Stones

Buty made its first Rediviva of the Stones in 2001, when Nina Buty's small, family-operated winery was the only Washington winery exploring premium Syrah and Cabernet–based blends. Today, this silky textured wine continues to set the standard for this core pairing. The grapes for the 2015 Rediviva of the Stones all came from the acclaimed Rocks District of Milton-Freewater appellation, which has emerged as one of the most coveted wine-growing regions in the state. With alluring violet and sassafras aromas, luscious fruit, and savory notes of smoked meat and cracked pepper, this is a dazzling wine alongside the most complex and truly unique of game dishes.

Elk Nacho Dip

Serves 4 to 6

This is a low-calorie dip with great southwestern flavor.

1 tablespoon olive oil
1 pound ground elk
½ onion, peeled and minced
Salt and cracked black pepper,
    to taste
1 (16-ounce) can refried beans
2 ounces chopped green chilies
1½ cups grated cheddar cheese
6 ounces mild taco salsa
3 chopped scallions
10 sliced ripe olives
1 cup sour cream, for garnish
1 cup guacamole, for garnish
Tostada chips

Preheat the oven to 400°F.

Heat the olive oil in a nonstick pan over medium heat until hot. Add the elk and onion and cook until the meat browns and the onion is soft. Season with salt and pepper.

Spread the refried beans in a flat 10-inch casserole dish. Layer the meat and onion over the beans. Sprinkle the chopped green chilies over the meat and onion. Cover with the cheese and salsa. Bake in the oven for 25 minutes. Remove from oven and sprinkle with the chopped scallions and olives. Before serving, garnish with sour cream and guacamole, and plenty of tostada chips.

WINE SUGGESTION:

2016 BEAST Wildebeest

Nina's BEAST wines have always been the alter ego of the winery's classic Buty wines, indulging a sense of exploration, while providing renowned winemaker Chris Dowsett the opportunity to create unique and dynamic wines with personalities all their own. The mercurial nature of these BEASTs allows Nina Buty and Chris the freedom to explore new varietals, new vineyards, and new blends. Made with a clear vision and voice, these wines have developed their own faithful following. Combining Syrah, Cabernet Sauvignon, and Cabernet Franc from Buty's Rockgarden Estate with grapes from the Phinny Hill and Conner Lee vineyards, this is a dynamic and delicious wine.

Braised Antelope Shoulder Roast

Serves 4 to 6

6 strips uncooked bacon

1 (3- to 5-pound) antelope chuck roast

½ cup all-purpose flour

½ cup vegetable oil

2 garlic cloves, peeled and minced

1 quart canned or fresh tomatoes, quartered

1 large onion, peeled and quartered

½ cup green pepper, seeded and chopped

2 teaspoons ground cumin

½ teaspoon salt

½ teaspoon cracked black pepper

Insert the bacon strips where the bones were removed from the roast. Close and bind with kitchen twine. Note: If the roast has already been rolled and tied, insert the bacon strips between the layers of the roll.

Dredge the roast in flour, and brown in hot oil in a large Dutch oven. Add garlic, tomatoes, onion, green pepper, cumin, salt, and pepper. Cover tightly and bring to a quick boil. Reduce the heat immediately and simmer slowly until the roast is tender, about 3 to 4 hours. Note: If you prefer to use an oven, cook the roast at 225°F until tender.

Remove the roast from the heat. Carve the roast and serve alongside noodles or rice, if desired.

WINE SUGGESTION:

2016 BEAST Phinny Hill Vineyard Cabernet Sauvignon

Made from 100 percent Cabernet, the core of this wine comes from a prized block at the top of Phinny Hill where stiff winds and rocky Spartan soils yield an alpha Cab, with glorious structure, robust tannins, and luxurious layers of fruit. And yet, because of the influence of the nearby river, and the cooling winds, this is also a beautifully dynamic BEAST that carries its power and weight with a graceful nonchalance. After twenty months in 30 percent new oak, it is strutting its signature Horse Heaven Hills perfumed aromatics, along with classic Cabernet flavors of black cherry, boysenberry, sweet tobacco leaf, woodsy cedar, and violet.

Chicken-Fried Antelope Steak

Serves 4

"I once spent several hours trying to invent the perfect chicken-fried steak. I used egg batters, beer batters, and every combination of spices I could contrive. Shortly thereafter, I stopped at Barbara Harris's Kozy Kottage Café in Kerrville, Texas. Having heard about her chicken-fried steak, I ordered one on a trial basis. It was as good as I have ever eaten. I knew there must be several secret herbs and spices involved, but I couldn't quite make them out. After I promised her fame and fortune, Barbara agreed to share her recipe with me."

—Mike Hughes, Founder, Broken Arrow Ranch

Vegetable oil or shortening, for frying
2 cups flour
Salt and cracked black pepper, as needed
2 pounds antelope or wild boar cutlets (4 to 6 ounces each)
2 cups buttermilk
Cream Gravy, as needed, recipe follows

In a deep, heavy skillet add oil/shortening to a depth of about 2 inches. Heat the oil to 350°F. Lightly season the flour with salt and pepper. Dip the cutlets in the buttermilk and then dredge in the seasoned flour. Repeat this process again. Working in small batches, cook the cutlets in the oil, turning once, until brown, about 4 or 5 minutes total. Transfer to a baking sheet lined with paper towels to drain. The cooked steaks can be kept warm in a 200°F oven while the remaining steaks are cooked and the Cream Gravy is prepared.

CREAM GRAVY

Pan drippings (from cooking the cutlets above)
4 tablespoons flour
2 cups milk
Salt and cracked black pepper, to taste

Pour off all but 4 tablespoons of the drippings from the pan. Be sure to leave all the crunchy little particles in the pan. Add an equal amount of flour and stir while browning over medium-high heat. Continue cooking slowly and stirring while adding the milk. (Note: It's much easier to thin the gravy by adding more milk than it is to thicken the sauce by adding more flour, so add the milk slowly until the desired consistency is reached.) Season with salt and pepper, to taste.

WINE SUGGESTION:

2014 Buty Columbia Rediviva, Phinny Hill Vineyard

While Buty's Rediviva of the Stones lets Syrah take the lead in the dance with Cabernet Sauvignon, in the Columbia Rediviva blend, Cabernet gets to shine, with Syrah playing a more supporting role. Grown on the east face of Phinny Hill by the Columbia River, the result is a wine with luxurious layers of perfume, black cherry, homemade strawberry jam, cranberry, and baking spices, as well as hints of peat, tea leaves, and spicy oak.

Herb-Crusted Antelope Filets with Horseradish Sauce

Serves 6 to 8

3 to 5 pounds boneless antelope loin (or boneless leg fillets)

2 tablespoons extra-virgin olive oil

Kosher salt, to taste

4 tablespoons Dijon mustard, divided

3 tablespoons cracked black peppercorns

2 tablespoons finely chopped fresh rosemary

2 tablespoons finely chopped fresh thyme

¼ cup sour cream

¼ cup mayonnaise

¼ cup prepared horseradish

Rub the loin with olive oil, then sprinkle a generous amount of salt over the loin. Next, rub the loin with 3 tablespoons of the mustard.

In a small bowl, combine the peppercorns, rosemary, and thyme. Mix well, then season the loin with the herb mixture. Cover or wrap the loin with plastic and allow to sit at room temperature for 1 hour. Alternatively, the loin can also be seasoned in advance and placed in the refrigerator; removing the loin 1 hour before cooking.

Preheat the oven to 425°F (or preheat an outdoor grill for direct, medium heat; page x).

Meanwhile, make the horseradish sauce by combining in a bowl the remaining 1 tablespoon mustard along with the sour cream, mayonnaise, and prepared horseradish. Mix well until smooth. Chill until ready to serve.

Roast or grill the loin to rare or medium-rare. For rare, remove the meat from the heat when the internal temperature from a meat thermometer reaches 115°F to 120°F, about 15 to 20 minutes total cooking time. For medium-rare, remove when internal temperature reaches 120°F to 125°F, about 20 to 25 minutes total cooking time. Remove from heat and let rest.

Slice the loin across the grain into ¼-inch medallions and serve with the horseradish sauce.

WINE SUGGESTION:

2015 Buty Conner Lee Vineyard Merlot & Cabernet Franc

A sophisticated and alluring blend from Buty—this one featuring Merlot and Cabernet Franc—is sourced exclusively from the sloping, sandy soils of the famed Conner Lee Vineyard. Planted in the early 1980s, Conner Lee is located at an elevation of approximately 1,125 feet, making it a cool site in a warm, sunny region. As a result, this wine combines bold, rich character with silky tannins, lovely energy, and complexity. It showcases layered aromas of ripe boysenberry, violet, chocolate-covered cherries, sage, and sweet clove, with a natural acidity that allows it to pair effortlessly with big meats and bold flavors.

South Texas Antelope Chuck Roast

Serves 4

1 (2- to 3-pound) antelope chuck roast

Steak seasoning, as needed (McCormick's)

3 tablespoons vegetable oil

1 onion, peeled and chopped

2 cups beef stock, divided

2 garlic cloves, peeled (or more to taste)

2 jalapeño peppers, seeded and chopped fine

1 can small dice tomatoes

2 green chilies, canned or fresh roasted and peeled, optional (if canned, add when 1 hour left to cook)

2 tablespoons tomato paste

1½ teaspoons dried oregano

2 tablespoons chili powder

1 tablespoon ancho chili powder

3 teaspoons cumin

¾ teaspoon salt (or more to taste)

⅛ teaspoon cracked black pepper

Preheat the oven to 225°F.

Season both sides of the roast liberally with the seasoning, making sure to pat it into the meat.

Add the oil to a Dutch oven over medium-high heat and brown the roast on all sides. Remove the roast and add the onion. Lower the heat to medium and cook until the onion is soft and slightly brown. Deglaze the pot with a little of the beef stock. Add the garlic and peppers and cook for about 1 minute with the onion. Return the roast to the pot with the lid. Pour the onion mixture on the top of the roast and add the can of tomatoes. In a separate bowl, combine the remaining beef stock with the fresh green chilies (if using), tomato paste, oregano, chili powders, cumin, salt, and pepper. Mix well and pour over the roast. Bring the pot to a simmer then transfer to the oven for 3 to 4 hours, or until the roast is very tender and falling apart. Note: Fork inserted into the meat should twist and "shred" the meat easily. Also, remember to add the canned green chilies, if using canned, when there is 1 hour left to cook.

After 2 hours, watch to make sure there is enough liquid in the pan to keep from burning. If needed, add a little water, but don't add too much. The mixture should become a thick, rich sauce.

Remove from oven. This is great served over Mexican rice with flour tortillas, salsa, and cubed avocado.

WINE SUGGESTION:

2014 BEAST Phinny Hill Vineyard "Reserva Style" Malbec

This is no meek and mild Malbec. In fact, in its youth, the Malbec from Buty's coveted section of Phinny Hill Vineyard in the Horse Heaven Hills can be so bold that Buty developed a "Reserva" program to tame its wild tannins. After twenty-one months in barrel and two years in bottle, this BEAST displays a regal, leonine power that exudes inky richness and potent flavors that can easily handle antelope and chilies, while still revealing the underlying complexity that makes this wine so special!

South Texas Antelope Summer Salad with Lemon Vinaigrette

Serves 4 to 5

Antelope is a very mild and lean meat that is well suited for summer dishes like this satisfying salad on a hot afternoon.

1 pound boneless antelope loin or fillets

Salt and cracked black pepper, to taste

1–2 heads romaine or green-leaf lettuce, cut into bite-size pieces

2–3 cups arugula

1 red onion, peeled and sliced

1–2 cups cherry tomatoes, halved (or beefsteak, sliced and quartered)

Gorgonzola, Parmesan, or crumbled goat cheese, as needed

Toasted pecans or walnuts, as needed, optional

Lemon Vinaigrette (recipe follows)

Preheat the oven to 425°F (or preheat an outdoor grill for direct, medium heat; page x).

Liberally season the antelope loin with salt and pepper. Roast or grill the loin to rare or medium-rare. For rare, remove the meat from the heat when the internal temperature from a meat thermometer reaches 115°F to 120°F. For medium-rare, remove when internal temperature reaches 120°F to 125°F. Remove from heat and let rest.

In a large bowl, add the lettuce, arugula, onion, tomatoes, cheese, and nuts. Drizzle with a little of the Lemon Vinaigrette over salad and toss.

To serve, arrange the salad among 4 or 5 serving plates. Thinly slice the loin across the grain and fan equal pieces on top of each salad.

LEMON VINAIGRETTE

½ cup red wine vinegar
1 cup olive oil
3 tablespoons lemon juice
2 teaspoons honey
2 teaspoons salt
Freshly ground black pepper,
    to taste

In a small bowl, whisk together the vinegar, oil, lemon juice, honey, salt, and pepper.

WINE SUGGESTION:

2016 Buty Conner Lee Vineyard Merlot & Cabernet Franc

Because 2016 yielded some of the most spectacular Cabernet Franc Buty had ever seen from the famed Conner Lee Vineyard, this gorgeous blend is a Cabernet Franc–driven wine. As a result, the nose displays alluring layers of red berries, cinnamon, ginger spice, and sweet cream, along with undercurrents of dusty cocoa. On the palate, jammy red fruit and floral notes mingle with savory hints of roasted red pepper coulis, making this an incredibly versatile red that shows what can be achieved from a great vineyard in a phenomenal vintage.

Roasted Wild Boar Leg with Mustard Caper Sauce

Serves 8 to 10

A wild boar leg can be cooked in the oven or in a pit using indirect heat. Be aware that wild pigs may be carriers of the trichina parasite, which means the meat must be cooked to a safe temperature before eating. Trichinosis is killed when the meat reaches a temperature of 137°F. Cooking tests have confirmed that cooking pork to a temperature of 150°F to 160°F results in not only a safe meat, but a more pleasing texture. Insert a meat thermometer into the thickest part of the leg and remove from the heat when the temperature reaches 150°F. Wild boar is a really lean meat, so it needs a sauce to add moisture.

1 (5- to 6-pound) bone-in boar leg
2 tablespoons olive oil
⅓ cup Dijon mustard
Mustard Caper Sauce, as needed, recipe follows

Remove the boar leg from the refrigerator and bring to room temperature (about 1 hour before cooking). Transfer the leg to a rack set in a large roasting pan.

Preheat the oven to 450°F.

In a small bowl, combine the olive oil and mustard and spread liberally all over the boar leg. Add a little water in the roasting pan and place in the oven. Roast for 20 minutes. Reduce the oven temperature to 275°F and continue cooking the leg until a meat thermometer inserted into the thickest part of the leg reads 150°F, about 4 to 5 hours.

Transfer the leg to a cutting board. Tent with foil and let rest for about 30 minutes before carving.

MUSTARD CAPER SAUCE

6 tablespoons butter

½ cup dry white wine

2 tablespoons Dijon mustard

½ teaspoon Worcestershire sauce

3 tablespoons capers, well drained

In a saucepan or pot, melt the butter over low heat. Mix in the wine, mustard, Worcestershire sauce, and capers. Stir to blend.

To serve, spoon the sauce over the sliced boar meat.

WINE SUGGESTION:

2014 Buty Rediviva of the Stones, Rockgarden Estate

Nina Buty planted her renowned, organically farmed Rockgarden Estate Vineyard specifically to make her acclaimed Rediviva of the Stones. Named for the famed basalt cobblestones that make this section of Walla Walla Valley so famous for wine growing. Rockgarden continues to yield an ever more complex wine each vintage, with beautiful structure, alluring aromatics, and zesty minerality. With layers of flowers, cinnamon, clove, roast game, and a hint of savory sesame oil and cracked black pepper, this is a tantalizing food wine that brings out the best from bold, robust dishes.

Wild Boar Porchetta

Serves 6 to 8

Is there anything better than roasted wild boar shoulder? Only if it's stuffed with sausage and herbs!

4 tablespoons olive oil

1 onion, peeled and thinly sliced

1 fennel bulb, thinly sliced

¾ pound Italian sausage (or wild boar Italian sausage)

2 tablespoons fennel seeds

2 tablespoons cracked black pepper

2 tablespoons fresh rosemary, chopped (or ½ tablespoon dried)

6 garlic cloves, peeled and chopped

Fennel leaves, chopped

2 eggs, beaten

4 pounds wild boar shoulder roast (or a rolled and tied wild boar leg)

Salt and pepper, to taste

4 cups vegetable mix, coarsely chopped (onion, celery, carrots, parsnips, etc.)

4 tablespoons butter, melted

4 tablespoons olive oil

In a large sauté pan over medium-high heat, add the olive oil. When hot, add the onion and fennel (bulb only). Cook until the onion is soft and translucent. Add the sausage, fennel seeds, pepper, rosemary, and garlic. Cook about 10 minutes, stirring frequently so the garlic does not burn. Allow the mixture to cool, then mix in the chopped fennel leaves and eggs.

Preheat the oven to 350°F.

Spread the mixture over one side of the wild boar, season with salt and pepper, then roll it up with a truss of kitchen twine. Spread the vegetable mixture on the bottom of a large roasting pan. Note: Use a mix of sturdy, savory vegetables to keep the wild boar off the bottom of the pan. Set the boar on top of the vegetable mix. Roast in the oven until the internal temperature reaches 150°F, about 2 to 2½ hours, basting every 20 to 30 minutes with melted butter and olive oil mixture. When done, remove from the oven and let rest for 15 to 20 minutes. Then slice thickly and serve.

WINE SUGGESTION:

2015 Buty Columbia Rediviva, Phinny Hill Vineyard

This wine comes exclusively from Phinny Hill Vineyard. Buty sought out its section of Phinny Hill specifically to make the Columbia Rediviva. The team also selected all of the trellising and pruning design for the Cabernet vines, with the Syrah planted to Nina's choice of clones. Planted on an east-facing slope of the hilltop, where they are protected from the Columbia River winds, year after year these vines yield a wine with gorgeous richness, structure, fruit, and spice. As a result, the Columbia Rediviva has regularly earned rave reviews and coveted spots on some of the most prestigious Top 100 lists in the world of wine.

Wild Boar Pozole

Serves 6 to 8

3 pounds wild boar, cleaned, trimmed, and cubed

Flour, as needed

Olive oil, as needed

3 quarts chicken or pork broth, divided

2 poblano chilies, roasted, peeled, seeded, and chopped, or 1 (7-ounce) can diced green chilies

3 (13-ounce) cans hominy, drained (white, yellow, or mixed)

1 medium onion, peeled and chopped

8 garlic cloves, peeled and minced

3 dried New Mexico (Anaheim) chilies, ground (or 2 tablespoons chili powder)

½ teaspoon dried oregano

½ teaspoon cracked black pepper

Salt, as needed

Sour cream, optional

Scallions, chopped, optional

Lightly coat the wild boar cubes with flour. Knock off any excess flour. In a large sauté pan or pot, heat some olive oil over medium-high heat. When hot, add the boar cubes in small batches, and brown on all sides. Once all the cubes are browned, deglaze the pan/pot with a small amount of broth, scraping up all the bits, and add this mixture to your cooking vessel.

Meanwhile, roast the poblano chilies: Broil the chilies 2 or 3 inches below the coils in a rimmed baking pan or roasting pan until the skins are nicely charred, about 7 minutes. Flip the chilies over and broil about 5 minutes longer until the other side is also charred. Remove from the oven and drape some foil over the chilies for about 10 minutes. This will make skinning the chilies much easier. Remove the skin, stems, and seeds, and discard. Rinse the chilies and then chop.

In a large pot or Dutch oven, add the wild boar cubes along with the hominy, onion, garlic, dried ground chilies, the roasted poblano chilies, oregano, pepper, and the remaining broth. Bring the mixture to a boil, then cover and gently simmer until the wild boar is fork-tender, about 2 hours. Add salt to taste.

Serve in bowls garnished with sour cream and chopped scallions, if desired.

WINE SUGGESTION:

2016 Buty Rockgarden Estate Mourvèdre, Syrah & Grenache

The defining feature of the Rocks District, where Buty's Rockgarden Estate is situated, is its cobblestone-rich gravel soils. The cobblestones possess numerous unique attributes that are ideal for growing wine grapes, including radiating heat that warms the clusters and influences the production of phenolic compounds during ripening, creating fascinating, profoundly aromatic wines with silky textures. Like Rhône meets the Rocks District, this Mourvèdre-based blend combines complex layers of meat, minerality, and black pepper with alluring layers of raspberry and strawberry.

Acknowledgments

The author would like to thank the following individuals and organizations for their assistance and support with this book:

Nicole Frail and Skyhorse Publishing; recipe consultant and food stylist Emily Lycopolus; food photographer Danielle Acken and DL Acken Photography; Ryan O'Hern and IGFC Bow, Washington; Devin Day and Valley Rabbits; Chris and Mike Hughes and Broken Arrow Ranch; Chef Aaron Tekulve; Mike Leventini; Matt Junkel and Scott Fortney and Petaluma Poultry; Chef Raymond Southern and Holly Southern; Chef John Ash; David Bottagaro and the National Pork Board; Keri Tawney and DeLille Cellars; Nina M. Buty and Buty Winery; Nicholas Berube and Grgich Hills Estate; Tess Sydlo and Wagner Vineyards; Raquel Royers and Clos Du Val Winery; Lilja Jonsson and Chateau St. Michelle Wine Estates; Miriam Pitt and J Lohr Vineyards & Wines, Ryan Johnson and King Estate Winery; Alex Thorkildsen and Mark Ryan Winery; Tiffany Armstrong; and last but not least, Bert Clay, for all the deliveries.

About the Author

James O. Fraioli is an accomplished cookbook author with a James Beard Award to his credit. He's published more than thirty celebrated culinary books, which have been featured on Food Network, *The Ellen DeGeneres Show*, Martha Stewart Living Radio, in *O, The Oprah Magazine*, *Vogue*, *Forbes*, the *Wall Street Journal*, and the *New York Times*. He's best known for teaming up with chefs, restaurants, mixologists, and industry professionals to showcase the best the culinary world has to offer. Prior to his successful culinary book publishing career, James served as a contributing writer and editor for dozens of food and wine magazine publications. He resides just outside Seattle, Washington. Visit him online at culinarybookcreations.com.

Conversion Charts

METRIC AND IMPERIAL CONVERSIONS
(These conversions are rounded for convenience)

Ingredient	Cups/Tablespoons/ Teaspoons	Ounces	Grams/Milliliters
Butter	1 cup/ 16 tablespoons/ 2 sticks	8 ounces	230 grams
Cheese, shredded	1 cup	4 ounces	110 grams
Cream cheese	1 tablespoon	0.5 ounce	14.5 grams
Cornstarch	1 tablespoon	0.3 ounce	8 grams
Flour, all-purpose	1 cup/1 tablespoon	4.5 ounces/0.3 ounce	125 grams/8 grams
Flour, whole wheat	1 cup	4 ounces	120 grams
Fruit, dried	1 cup	4 ounces	120 grams
Fruits or veggies, chopped	1 cup	5 to 7 ounces	145 to 200 grams
Fruits or veggies, pureed	1 cup	8.5 ounces	245 grams
Honey, maple syrup, or corn syrup	1 tablespoon	0.75 ounce	20 grams
Liquids: cream, milk, water, or juice	1 cup	8 fluid ounces	240 milliliters
Oats	1 cup	5.5 ounces	150 grams
Salt	1 teaspoon	0.2 ounce	6 grams
Spices: cinnamon, cloves, ginger, or nutmeg (ground)	1 teaspoon	0.2 ounce	5 milliliters
Sugar, brown, firmly packed	1 cup	7 ounces	200 grams
Sugar, white	1 cup/1 tablespoon	7 ounces/0.5 ounce	200 grams/12.5 grams
Vanilla extract	1 teaspoon	0.2 ounce	4 grams

OVEN TEMPERATURES

Fahrenheit	Celsius	Gas Mark
225°	110°	¼
250°	120°	½
275°	140°	1
300°	150°	2
325°	160°	3
350°	180°	4
375°	190°	5
400°	200°	6
425°	220°	7
450°	230°	8

Index

Recipe Index